THE EVOLUTION

of

CONCEPTUAL ART

in

AMERICA

The Evolution of Conceptual Art in America

by

Kempton Mooney

FKM Books
New York

Contents

1. Introduction

In 1965, conceptual art came into use as a term defining art with primary importance placed on the artists' propositional concept, de-emphasizing the manner of execution. Conceptual art as a popular phenomenon, known as conceptualism, had a profound impact upon the art world as a whole because it could manifest itself in any material or form. This allowed conceptual artists to approach themes that artists working in traditional materials could not. The term conceptual art was defined by Sol LeWitt, a pioneer of the movement, to describe diverse forms of written and visual documentation, including textual data, diagrams, drawings, maps, and photographic records. Stressing the use of language and thought process, the movement was the culmination of written information being enacted as art, something begun early in the century.

In minimizing the relevance of the permanent visual object, conceptual art also demonstrated a disappointment with the museum and gallery system. It brought forth issues such as art as a commodity, what art could be, and art's role in society. It set out to shock the art community, to change the language of art, and to introduce a new way of perceiving and discussing art. Though it produced few known master works, conceptualism is credited with breaking from conventional art-making and did a great deal to open up the art world. This paper, focusing on conceptualism in the United States, will investigate the degree to which conceptual art accomplished what it set forth to do.

To determine if the conceptualists' ideas broke with tradition and influenced the direction of art, this paper will examine the art world from which conceptualism came, define how it differed from its background, and explain the results of the conceptual art movement. First, this paper will look at the greater art scene in the United States that preceded it. This will produce an overall context in which to place conceptual art and demonstrate that it did not break with what came before it, but was instead the next logical step in a progression. Then the goals of major artists who contributed heavily to conceptualism will be delineated. Their works will be analyzed, investigating them in reference to each other and to what critics, such as Robert Morgan, Ursula Meyer, and Lucy Lippard have written about them. The paper will then examine how conceptual art declined in the mid-1970's and later gained in popularity.

2. Defining Conceptual Art

There have been many definitions of conceptual art given by artists and critics. This section will explain the idea of conceptual art, looking at a number of these definitions and differentiating the methodology from the movement that has been dubbed conceptualism.

Conceptualism looked to early academies that established fine art as a learned, self-conscious activity in Western culture. One of these tenets was a mistrust of the optical as a basis for art. Like Marcel Duchamp, many conceptualists believed the more painting relied on purely visual sensation, "the lower its cognitive value was assumed to be."[1] Late in the nineteenth century, the avant-garde had successfully turned academia on its head, freeing sensual immediacy of color and texture from an imposed intellectual program. Conceptual art's de-emphasis on purely visual sensations marked an end to this strategy. However, subsequent theories have strengthened conventional attachments to painting and sculpture as the art market functions more comfortably selling these objects.

There are a few distinctions that need to be made. As multiple artists and critics have defined conceptual art, many critics, out of convenience, now apply the term to works and processes to which the term does not apply. Of

---

[1] Crow, Thomas, *Modern Art in the Common Culture*, New Haven, 1996, 215.

the multiple definitions, none describes all of conceptual art, but instead, all pieces fit the definitions to various degrees. What I will be referring to when I use the term is art wherein the conceptual aspect is more important than the physical object that represents it.[2] This means that while a purely conceptual work would be simply an idea with no material manifestation, a work of conceptual art may be communicated through a painting, a photo, a model, a map, a text, or any other form of documentation the artist uses to convey the concept which is the basis of the work. Lawrence Weiner's works are an excellent example. Weiner created statements, such as "One quart exterior green enamel thrown on a brick wall."[3] By simply thinking this idea, he created what he called a sculpture. To communicate the idea to others, he could write it on paper, speak it, or draw a diagram. But these forms of communication are not necessary for the work of art to exist, as the idea is the essence of the work. This method of art was a popular phenomenon from the mid-sixties to the mid-seventies across the globe. However, as Lucy Lippard has noted, it was not a unified movement as the artists worked independently. The surge in popularity of a method or process critical towards primarily visual art has been titled conceptualism by critics as a large umbrella to cover all the works appearing to focus primarily upon the art idea. The distinction between the movement and method is far from precise "and frequently breaks down in the works of artists who deliberately crossed genres and media forms."[4]

Artists whose works fall under the umbrella of conceptual and have had a significant impact upon the art world have been dubbed the conceptualists. Though there are many rosters of many lengths that define artists as conceptualists, here is a small, general list of those working in the United States: the Art and Language group, John Baldassari, Robert Barry, Mel Bochner, Daniel Buren, Victor Burgin, John Cage, Jan Dibbets, Hans Haacke, General

---

[2] LeWitt, Sol, "Paragraphs on Conceptual Art" in Harrison and Wood, *Art in Theory: 1900-1990*, Oxford, 1998, 834.

[3] Godfrey, Tony, *Conceptual Art*, London, 1998, 165.

[4] Bird and Newman, *Rewriting Conceptual Art*, London, 1999, 6.

Idea, Dan Graham, Douglas Huebler, On Kawara, Joseph Kosuth, Les Levine, Sol LeWitt, Richard Long, Robert Morris, Bruce Nauman, Dennis Oppenheim, Adrian Piper, Bernar Venet, and Lawrence Weiner.[5]

The term conceptual art has a debatable origin, but it is generally believed that it came into popular use between 1965 and 1967. Before this, Ed Keinholz had alluded to the idea of conceptual art in his essays of the late 1950's. Henry Flynt, in 1961, described a type of concept art in which the materials were the concepts, similar to music, in which the materials are sounds. Duchamp also spoke of something similar as "brain facts" early in the century to emphasize the intellectual rather than physical aspects of art. Robert Morgan believes that conceptual art has been with us since 1913, when Duchamp made his first readymade and Malevich made his first suprematist painting.

Conceptual art challenged the traditional idea of the art object as a unique, collectable commodity. It did so by suggesting that the quality that makes an object a work of art exists only in the viewer's mind and through his mental participation. The viewer takes on an active, rather than passive, role as receiving the work becomes part of the work. In this way, conceptual art explored the mechanics of meaning.

Conceptual art also offers a critique of art, questioning why we have needed the object in the past. Many artists, such as Lawrence Weiner, Robert Barry, and Joseph Kosuth, saw themselves as taking art past the object into the realm of language. This critique has had a profound effect on contemporary artists.

To question art, as conceptual art has done, is to question the materialistic values of our culture and society. It demonstrates dissatisfaction with the gallery system and questions ownership by reducing the ownable object to mere documentation. In today's culture, the museum is a church, where the congregated meditate on icons in a quiet hush. The object is fetishized without thought as to why. Conceptual art has tried to raise awareness of this event by questioning the necessity of the object in worship. Art became simply information, not to be judged by

[5] Atkins, Robert, *Artspeak*, New York, 1997, 74.

aesthetics, as Doug Huebler said, but on its interest as an idea.[6] Artists became concerned with issues of communication, documentation, meaning, and these issues were central to the art because they were the ideas expressed.

While conceptual art has always been considered to be an international phenomenon, it has been described as disseminating out of New York, the self-proclaimed center of the art world in the sixties and seventies. However, a recent exhibition called *Global Conceptualism* offered a different proposal: that conceptual art surfaced in many different nations around the world independently. Artists would have been influenced by each other and by the same sources, such as Duchamp, but developed for the most part on their own. Their different backgrounds and the diversity of local cultures shaped conceptual art differently in places such as Japan and Eastern Europe, for example. I think conceptual art in America is different from conceptual art in Western Europe or Australia, even though artists in these areas would have corresponded and interacted. Michael Newman and Jon Bird call this conceptual art's "local specificity and its global reach."[7] Too much emphasis has been placed on the New York scene being a core of conceptual art as a global phenomenon and not enough attention has been paid to how conceptual art in America developed in itself.

A common issue is how to recognize conceptual art if it is not defined by a medium or style. Works of conceptual art have taken many forms: readymades, interventions (objects in unexpected contexts), documentation (works presented by evidence), and language. And though the definitions of conceptual art number as many as the artists themselves, one main guideline is that the idea of the work is of primary importance while the object that is created, if there is one, is of secondary importance. Many conceptual works are reflexive, starting with the question, "What is art?" and ending with the answer that this actual questioning is art. These artists doubt the traditions around them

---

[6] Huebler, Doug, "Saboteur or Trophy? Advance or Retreat?" *Artforum*, v. 20 no. 9, May 1982, 76.

[7] Bird and Newman, *Rewriting Conceptual Art*, London, 1999, 1.

and imagine what could be. They say art of the future does not have to look like art of the past.[8] Similarly, Kosuth defined conceptual art as inquiring into the foundations of the concept of art,[9] but during the seventies many other conceptual artists disdainfully viewed Kosuth's theoretical art as self-absorbed. Lippard discusses in *Six Years* the importance of the dematerialization of the object, which many other critics of the time, such as Jack Burnham, saw as a gimmick.[10] Since she wrote the book in 1973, Lippard has suggested that the term "dematerialization" is inadequate for describing the increasing conceptualization of art. Though many of those who stressed the importance of dematerializing have retracted, some are adamant, such as Michael Kirby, who describes conceptual art as striving towards the absence of the physical, though conceptualists knew it was impossible.[11] These challenges to its defining characteristics demonstrate the controversial nature of defining conceptual art.

One last defining characteristic of conceptualism is its reaction to formalism with a return to focusing on content and meaning. By the 1960's, the dominant strain of modernism was formalism, which focused solely on the use of new and more appropriate styles developed to represent the new world of industrialization and mass media. Modernism concerned itself with the visual elements that give a work its form: shape, structure, size, scale, composition, etc. "Formalism is generally believed to imply an artistic or interpretive emphasis on form, rather than content, but form and content are, in fact, complementary aspects in any work."[12] A uniting element of conceptual art is its re-

---

[8] Clegg and Guttmann, "On Conceptual Art's Tradition," *Flash Art*, v. XXI no. 143,

Nov./Dec., 1988, 99.

[9] Godfrey, Tony, *Conceptual Art*, London, 1998, 13.

[10] Lippard, Lucy R., *Six Years: The Dematerialization of the Art Object from 1966 to 1972*, New York, 1973.

[11] Kirby, Michael, "Foreword," in Robert D. Morgan, *Conceptual Art: An American Perspective*, London, 1994, IX.

[12] Atkins, Robert, *Artspeak*, New York, 1997, 98.

action against formalism. Kosuth saw formalist art as an art condition. He believed that it was called art because it resembled work that came before it, i.e. a canvas in a certain shape and size stained a certain way with such a color. This view leads to a predetermined idea of the possibilities of art. Formalist art critics accepted a definition of art based on formal characteristics. This posed a problem to conceptualists because many objects or images may appear similar, but this does not mean that they are related in an artistic or conceptual relationship. Therefore, formalist criticism analyzed the physical attributes of particular objects that happen to exist in a context. This did little to add to the understanding of a work of art overall, as it does not investigate the idea structure that drove the work and gave many twentieth century pieces, such as readymades, their complexity. So in reaction to this, conceptualists believed it was important to try to understand, though it may be impossible, the nature of art, and expand it. Questioning the nature of art is a major tenet that conceptual art traces back to Duchamp through a complex network of art historical roots.

3. Precursors

Art that exists solely as ideas seems an extreme notion and even today is met with skepticism. However, the emergence of conceptualism was not a sudden radical break, but was a recognition and popularization of ideas that already existed. To decipher where conceptual art comes from involves trying to distinguish who did what first, over which there is great dispute. One could write an entire history of the importance of the idea in the work of art. Some examples are Van Eyck's self-portrait and Magritte's *Ceci n'est pais une pipe*. Van Eyck's self-portrait contains at the top of the work the phrase "to the best of my ability," which seems very modest, but the painting is masterfully executed. The work contains self-referral and illuminates issues of meaning and issues in the signifier-signified relationship.

Magritte's *Ceci n'est pais une pipe* has similar issues, though made centuries later, dating from 1926. It juxtaposes a picture of a smoking pipe with the words "This is not a pipe" written in French below it. Again, there is paradox in the signifier-signified relationship, and a theme of self-reference. These works both contain aspects that appeal to the viewer's mind rather than his eye. They are examples of singular works in history that contain the seed of what would become conceptual art.

There is an adage in playwriting that for a gun to be fired at someone in the third act of a play, it must be shown in act one and loaded in act two. Duchamp and dada were the act one that allowed neo-dada and minimalists to load the gun which conceptual art fired. The ideas of Duchamp and other artists had been incorporated into the American art scene long enough to produce a number of artists who, contemporary and independent of each other, utilized the medium of the idea.

Duchamp's readymades state that they are art, and in doing so question for the first time what makes something a work of art. But, before Duchamp, Picasso's collage painting of chair caning does something similar: it is at the same time representational and the real thing. The letters "JOU" refer to "*journal*" or newspaper. The word is linked to reality, but is itself painted and not material reality.[13] So cubists introduced the everyday object as part of a work of art before Duchamp's readymade, but it is the readymade that introduced the everyday object itself as art. By referring to the everyday object, both disrupt the viewer's idea and ask the viewer how he or she knows what he or she knows. Later, the conceptual art of the sixties would employ the same technique -the use of the everyday- to shock the viewer and force critical thinking.

Although Marcel Duchamp was associated with both dadaism and surrealism, he began his career associated with cubism. However, in 1912, his *Nude Descending a Staircase (No. 2)* was removed from a cubist exhibit as it did not fit the hanging committee's idea of what a cubist painting should be, as it resembled futurism too closely. Duchamp realized the avant-garde, once accepted, could be just as tyrannical as the academies.[14] Duchamp desired to put art "in the service of the mind," but after his fiasco with the cubists, he believed painting could not do so. For this reason, he would later give up painting for chess. He began to claim chess as his artistic medium, chess containing the mental effort that defined art. His interest in chess stemmed from his interest in logic and his desire to educate his audience about the limits of reason. He saw painting as physical and with no notion of free thought, as it was governed by rules of aesthetics. So he began his fight

---

[13] Godfrey, Tony, *Conceptual Art*, London, 1998, 24.

[14] Ibid., 27.

against what he called "retinal art," art which appealed to the eye through beauty.

Duchamp desired to shock, to question the authority that could not define the perimeters of art, but dictated what objects should be considered art. He said later, "I was interested in ideas, not merely visual products."[15] For him, a work of art would be an object in the physical world and more importantly, what he would call a "brain fact." His readymades were examples of these brain facts. He described them as objects taken from the "everyday world and deprived ... of all functional, technical, and commercial value."[16] In doing so, however, he gave them a new function: to develop ideas through artistic status. Duchamp said it was useless to define a work of art except as a mental effort, as a victory over taste.

Duchamp's readymades, such as *The Fountain*, were a victory over taste as they wre not chosen ofr their aesthetic qualities. They begged the viewer to ask what are the conditions for making a work of art. *The Fountain* was a urinal Duchamp bought at the J.L. Mott Ironworks and submitted to the Society of Independent Artists' first exhibition in 1917 under the false name R. Mutt. The exhibition was to have no jury; any artist who paid the six dollar entrance fee could show. Duchamp submitted *The Fountain* to see if the directors of the Society would stick to their word. William Glacken, the president of the Society, was horrified and said the urinal was indecent and could not be shown, unaware that it was Duchamp who had submitted it. The directors quickly voted that the work would not be exhibited, explaining to the press that it was by no means a work of art. The work began a debate over who determined something was a work of art, testing the "standards and behavior of the Society's directors."[17] And as *The Fountain* had been for sale before the directors had pulled it from the exhibit, it raised questions of commodity and originality. Why does a commodity, because of the labor put into it by someone like Duchamp, become

---

[15] Ibid.

[16] Ibid.

[17] Ibid., 30.

something that is above its use value? This investigation of commodity worship demonstrates a concern with fetishism that conceptual artists would confront through the dematerializing of the art object.

The division between the retinal and the conceptual was a central element in Duchamp's work. Though other works in the past have stated they were art, his readymades were the first that in doing so questioned what makes something art. He was the first artist in western tradition to place more value upon the conceptual component of a work than on the visual. This was the first step in the production of an art whose medium was simply the idea, and that is why he is considered to be the father of conceptual art.

Duchamp was a father figure to the dadaists as well as to the conceptualists. But dadaists and conceptualists also drew from the use of language in cubist collages. In cubist pieces, it was not that the words themselves were the art, but the cubists' use of words acknowledged the everyday and, like a readymade, raised questions as to what could be used in art. Francis Picabia's dada painting *The Cacodylic Eye,* from 1921, is an example of how the dadaists later appropriated the cubist use of text. *The Cacodylic Eye* consists of messages which visitors to the artist's apartment had painted on the canvas. This piece deconstructed painting with its non-traditional composition. It did not express the artist's personality, but was instead a place for people to meet, a compendium of their ideas. This piece used text to question ideas of art, ownership, and authorship, and embodied what would be a tenet of conceptualism, that the idea, here the collaboration of the artist with his visitors, is the machine that drives the artwork. It also recognized that the art of the future did not have to look like the art of the past, and it did so with the independence and rejection of tradition typical of dada.

Apart from Duchamp, dada was concentrated mostly in Europe. In 1916, Hugo Ball founded dada at the Cabaret Voltaire in Zurich as a protest against World War I, desiring to remind the world that there are independent men who will stand up for their ideals.[18] "What we call

---

[18] Ball, Hugo, "Dada Fragments" (1916-1917), translation from Harrison and Wood, *Art in Theory: 1900-1990,* p. 247.

Dada is a harlequinade made of nothingness in which all higher questions are involved ... The Dadaist loves the extraordinary, the absurd even... The Dadaist fights against the death-throes and death-drunkenness of his time." [19] Tristan Tzara, who edited the French magazine *Dada*, wrote in the "Dada Manifesto of 1918," "I write a manifesto and I want nothing, yet I say certain things and in principle I am against manifestoes ... I write this manifesto to show that people can perform contrary actions... I do not explain because I hate common sense." [20] This demonstrates the militant nature of dada, which it coupled with a desire for freedom, anarchy, and chaos. "Dada was born of a need for independence, of a distrust for unity. Those who are with us preserve their freedom. We recognize no theory." [21] There was a great desire for social change combined with a vehement message that they wanted nothing: dada was full of contradictions. "The Dadaist is naïve... The Dadaist considers it necessary to come out against art, because he has seen through its fraud as a moral safety valve. Perhaps this militant attitude is a last gesture of inculcated honesty, perhaps it merely amuses the Dadaist, perhaps it means nothing at all." [22] Overall, dada was more concerned with promoting anarchy, personal freedom, and the destruction of logic than with the production of art objects.

Walter Benjamin in his "The Author as Producer" described dada's strength as testing art's authenticity.[23] It did so "to the extent that it sacrificed the market values which are so characteristic of the [work] in favor of higher ambitions."[24] Their works' promotion of the irrational was more important to the dadaists than their sales values. They also challenged the notion of what materials could be

---

[19]Ibid.

[20] Tzara, Tristan, "Dada Manifesto 1918" (1918), in Harrison and Wood, *Art in Theory: 1900-1990,* p. 249.

[21] Ibid., 250.

[22] Huelsenbeck, Richard, *En Avant Dada* (1920), in Harrison and Wood, *Art in Theory: 1900-1990,* p. 258.

[23] Benjamin, Walter, "The Author as Producer" (1934), in Harrison and Wood, *Art in Theory: 1900-1990,* 1998, 486.

used in art. "Dadaistic activities actually assured a rather vehement distraction by making works of art the center of scandal. One requirement was foremost: to outrage the public."[25] An example of their desire to shock the audience, as Duchamp had done, is Ben Peret's 1926 insulting priests on the street, documented by photographs. The work was the action of insulting the priest, illogical and destructive, but promoting freedom at the same time. The photo was not the art but was evidence of the art having taken place, and by using documentation such as this, artists were able to present more things as art than in the past. However, problems arose from using documentation, such as distinguishing the documentation from the art itself, and these later problems would plague the conceptualists. The conceptualists did not invent this idea of documenting works that enabled the artists to present more things as art than in the past. It was instead a continuance of the techniques already established by the dadaists.

Often times dadaists works had to be assigned to separate rooms once a curator saw the nature of the pieces. This occurred in 1919 to Max Ernst and Johannes Baargeld in a show at the Cologne Kunstverein. Ernst and Baargeld subsequently decided to show, along with their works, readymades, such as an umbrella and a piano hammer, and works by children in their room.[26] The staging of the exhibition, rather than any particular element, became the artwork. Ernest Baurgeld held an exhibitionin 1920 in the Brasserie Winter in Cologne that told the viewer to go and destroy what he did not like. This deconstructed the bourgeois exhibition, where the people are told what they will like as art, and this deconstuction prefigures conceptual art's attention to how art is exhibited.

The dadaists' emphasis on their ideas and philosophies rather than their material work demonstrates the conceptual quality of dada. Some critics, such as Godfrey, view conceptual art as developing from Duchamp in waves,

[24] Benjamin, Walter, "The Work of Art in the Age of Mechanical Reproduction" (1936), in Harrison and Wood, *Art in Theory: 1900-1990*, 1998, 517.

[25] Ibid.

[26] Ibid., 44.

dada being the first wave of development.[27] According to this view, dada was an early phase of conceptual art. However, Duchamp was not the only father figure to conceptualists. Many, including Kosuth, were greatly influenced by the teachings of Ad Reinhardt.

Coming to painting with a background in art history and philosophy, Ad Reinhardt had the tools to create a completely introspective art. He emphasized the tautological nature of art in his paintings as he gradually tried to remove the anti-art qualities from his work. By 1950, he was painting clean and linear paintings with varying shades of one predominate color. In the late fifties, he began to paint all black works. The paintings were five-feet square divided into nine sections. In purifying his paintings, he had eliminated color, brush strokes, texture and everything that was not art. He chose a size that was not big or small; it simply existed. He would not vary from this pure format for the rest of his life.

Reinhardt's works demonstrated his belief that "art is art as art and everything else is everything else. Art as art is nothing but art."[28] He hated subjectivity, and instead desired total introspection in art. He believed art should be detached, empty, and "immaterial."[29] This meant no lines or images, shapes or symbols, no decorating, no accidents or readymades, no things, no relations, no attributes, nothing that was not of the essence.[30] In support of his ideas, he not only painted, but lectured and wrote continuously, assigning meaning to his black paintings and making it hard for critics to co-opt it. This would impress upon future artist such as Joseph Kosuth that the total activity of the artist gave works a cultural life. It became the artist's responsibility to discuss art theory. Reinhardt fathered not only abstract painting, but also the idea of whittling art down to pure introspection.

---

[27] Ibid., 37.

[28] Reinhardt, Ad, "Art as Art" (1962), in Harrison and Wood, *Art in Theory: 1900-1990*, 1998, 805.

[29] Ibid., 809.

[30] Ibid., 808.

After World War II, there was a great desire in America, as well as in Europe, for the materialism, civility, and culture of the visual arts. As a result, there was not a demand for revolutionary art, but for visual images. Painting reigned. However, while there was not a great counter-movement, there were individuals who fought against the tyranny of accepted painting. Individuals such as John Cage, Robert Rauschenberg, Jasper Johns, and the choreographer Merce Cunningham desired to revive the ideas of Duchamp and the dadaists. They questioned traditional assumptions about art and the art object.

Before the war, Cage, a composer, was already known for his experimental work and rejection of the traditional European notions of form and composing. In the fifties, he created pieces such as *4'33"*, a piano concerto in three movements in which the pianist sits at a piano silently for four minutes and thirty-three seconds. The audience is meant to observe silence and the everyday noises, which fill the background wash of silence. Any sound could be music. At the center of Cage's work, like the work of the dadaists, was a belief in personal freedom and a rejection of value judgements. To him, everything could be considered beautiful if conceived of properly. It was the idea, the recognition, and the perspective of the viewer that made a work interesting.

After World War II, Rauschenberg's work progressed from photography to the utilization of found objects in paintings, heavily influenced by Duchamp and the dadaists. During this time he worked with Cage, Johns, and Cunningham at Black Mountain College in North Carolina and with them began what they described as "happenings," performance events that empowered the viewer and helped art escape the museum. In 1953, Rauschenberg sold white paintings, and knowing they would become dirty, arranged to have them repainted by someone years later. This questioned ideas of originality, authorship, and the fetish value of culture, placing value on a work because of the labor put into it. It was not important that Rauschenberg painted the canvas; what was important was what he revealed through the absence of imagery. This focus on the absence of imagery is also seen in his drawing in reverse, in which he took a drawing by Willem de Kooning, whom he admired greatly, and erased the drawing, leaving a smudged and almost blank piece of paper. The art critic Leo Steinberg asked Rauschenberg if he, Steinberg, would better appreciate the *Erased de Kooning* having actually viewed it, to which Rauschenberg said no, suggesting that art could be the idea, not simply a physical fact. The happenings, the reverse drawing, and the white canvases demonstrate Rauschenberg's disdain for tradition and desire to broaden the definition of art. In these works, the process and idea of the work, not the actual object, are important.

Johns, like Rauschenberg, was interested in the use of everyday objects. His paintings of flags, targets, and numbers from the 1950's have illustrated the role of intention in defining a work of art. His gestural brushstrokes seem to suggest a personal expression, like abstract expressionist work, yet the image seems to negate this idea. The image instead seems to comment on the "philosophical dilemmas concerning the language of art and the perception of reality."[31]   Duchamp's influence is apparent in his 1968 set design for Merce Cunningham, which was designed after Duchamp's *Large Glass*. His works such as *Painted Bronze* of 1950, two cast cans of ale, demonstrate the influence Duchamp's readymades had on him. Johns was also described as pop; his ale can bronzing was a demonstration that popular art dealers could sell anything, even a pair of beer cans. He, with Rauschenberg, desired to show anything could be considered art. Their use of unconventional material required the viewer to think about art, what made something art, and in doing so set a precedent for freedom of material and method in art.

The term neo-dada was first applied to Rauschenberg, Johns, Allan Kaprow and Cy Twombly in 1958 in *Art-News*, and later to Ed Kienholz.[32] Neo-dada used objects not to challenge art, but to make them art. They rejected much of the aggressive attitude of original dada and did not try to impose social change. They tried instead to re-

---

[31] Fineberg, Jonathan, *Art Since 1940: Strategies of Being*, Upper Saddle River, 1995, 208.

[32] *ArtNews*, v. 56, Jan. 1958, 5. Atkins, Robert, *Artspeak*, New York, 1997, 128.

discover dada, using its tradition to give them the freedom to put the world together in unique ways.

Ed Kienholz was pigeonholed as a neo-dadaist because he, like Rauschenberg, was creating large combine paintings in the fifties. At the beginning of the sixties he began creating works in the form of large scale environments. However, he found the cost of producing these environments expensive and that what was important was the idea of the work. So instead of continuing to create these large scale pieces, he simply wrote the instructions for the work and sold the concept. One could either buy the concept from him, commission a drawing of the concept, or commission the realization of the concept in full scale. Some have called these the first true conceptual works. Tony Godfrey says they are not because Kienholz simply stopped producing the full-scale works out of necessity.[33] I contend it is both, that even though he stopped full scale production out of lack of funds, these circumstances lead him to a medium less expensive, that of ideas. However, he did not believe the art object was devoid of value, as he did continue to produce objects. He simply realized that works of art are not dependent on objects.

Contemporary with the neo-dadaists were Piero Manzoni and Yves Klein in Europe. Both have been described as actionists, along with Joseph Beuys, and as *nouveau realistes*. Their philosophical action works as well as their paintings set a precedent for conceptual art in America and especially body art, an offshoot of conceptual art. Klein, at the age of sixteen, was already creating revolutionary pieces such as his *Symphonie Monoton,* which consisted of a single note. Works like *Symphonie Monoton* questioned what art could be. Another such work was his *Le Vide* exhibition of 1958, which consisted of an empty gallery in Paris to give the viewer a feeling of empty space. The work symbolized the Rosicrucian belief that art's real importance was beyond sight and sound.[34] After two years he produced his "Anthropometries," paintings made by in-

---

[33] Godfrey, Tony, *Conceptual Art,* London, 1998, 92.

[34] The Rosicrucians were a religious organization that believed images and colors had specific spiritual associations. For example, blue was the color of the sky and the spirit.

structing nude models to cover themselves with Klein Blue paint and imprint themselves on the canvas. He invited an audience to view the event, as the process was part of the work of art. Though he continued to make works that had a personal touch and were easily recognizable, Klein was also looking towards the more spiritual, using unusual techniques and materials to convey ideas in new ways. His efforts to broaden the parameters of art are exemplified in the tittle of a lecture he gave at the Sorbonne: "The Evolution of Art Towards the Immaterial."[35]

The Italian artist Manzoni desired to link the individual with art and the artist, having a huge impact on the way conceptual art developed in America and in Europe. He himself was heavily influenced by dada and the futurists. Fascinated with the public's fetish for anything produced by the artist, he began to sign small objects as art, such as cans containing his own excrement, and sealed cans which contained a rolled piece of paper marked with a single line. These works came complete with certificates of authenticity, as did his signing of friends and models as living readymades. One of his living readymades was Marcel Broodthaers who was then a poet. Manzoni, though independent of Klein, was greatly influenced by Klein's monochrome paintings. After seeing a Klein exhibition, Manzoni began his series of *Achromes*, which where also monochrome works. He gave these works texture, using medium from paint and plaster to cottonballs and pebbles mounted on canvas. His use of unusual media, his interest in the public's fetish with the art object, and his demonstration that the artist had become an icon had a powerful impact on many of the conceptualists. Manzoni, though typically classified as a *nouveau realiste*, is more purely conceptual and innovative than many conceptualists. He is a clear example of the existence of conceptual art before conceptualism took hold, and demonstrates that conceptual art was more of an evolution of a medium than a movement.

The tremendous influence Manzoni had on the art world can be demonstrated in describing the works of Marcel Broodthaers. Broodthaers started out as a Belgian

---

[35] Hunter, Sam and John Jocabus, *Modern Art*, New York, 1992, 360.

poet connected to the *surrealisme–revolutionaire* move-ment. Concerned with ideological, social, and political is-sues, the *surrealisme-revolutionaire* was founded by Chris-tian Dotremont, the "moving spirit of various small groups which he united in a powerful international move-ment."[36] Through this group, Broodthaers was in contact with artists, but the experience of Manzoni signing him as a living readymade in 1963 turned him towards art. The next year he began writing critiques of contemporary American artists, as well as producing his first art objects and pictorial works. His objection to commercialist trends in art led to his founding the fictitious Musee d'Art Mod-erne in 1968, which manifested itself in venues such as his house and other locales around him. In 1970, he created his virtual museum on a Belgian beach by tracing its floor plan in the sand. He and a colleague, dressed in uniform, set up signs which told visitors not to touch the art ob-jects, only to have the museum washed away by the tide. Though not an American, he was a conceptualist connec-ted to the American art scene through his criticism.

Just as there was a climate of unrest in politics during the sixties, there was a similar feeling of unrest in the art scene, probably fueled by the social climate. There was dis-satisfaction with the institutionality of the art world, in-cluding academies, galleries, museums, and funding. There was also discontent with traditional forms of expression. Artists used self-criticism in an attempt to purify art, which meant self-definition and freedom from oppressive tradition.

A direct example of disappointment in the art estab-lishments was Claus Oldenberg's *The Store*. Oldenberg created small physical objects in great numbers and then rented a street front store and sold the objects in the store. But it was not just the objects that were art. The store it-self was one of Oldenberg's pieces, whether those who me-andered through it knew it or not. *The Store* demon-strated a disappointment in the gallery system of New York by avoiding the galleries altogether. Oldenberg's sub-ject was taken from the street in a way similar to pop art,

---

[36] *Art Since Mid-Century: The New Internationalism,* with contributions by Werner Haftmann (and others), Greenwich, 1971, 70.

an abbreviation for the popular art that appeared in the early sixties. Lawrence Alloway first coined the term popular art as a reference to work which used popular culture and advertising images as subjects. But Oldenberg's interest in paradox separated him from the pop movement. His preference for the appearance of the gesture rather than mechanical reproduction also separated him from pop. He created works depicting everyday subjects, but did so with an exaggerated, artist's hand. He would later parody everyday products by depicting them in a ridiculously large format and in a range of various materials. This exploration of medium would later be a theme throughout the careers of several conceptualists.

Happenings were one technique used to take authority from the institution and give authority directly to the participants. But while these happenings were supposed to be about emancipation and the empowerment of the participant, often times the happenings had an agenda, which seems counter intuitive to their purpose. George Brecht, an organizer of happenings, often had less of an agenda. Instead, he would leave an object out for viewers to examine and with which to toy. He sent cards to his friends containing instructions such as to observe a sign to travel in a direction and travel in that direction. This technique of using instructions came to be seen as a form of conceptual art, for an idea was communicated with the potential for the participant to experience a revelation.

Warhol was the paradigm of pop art, taking the commodification of the art object literally and decided that 100 images would be better than one. Warhol began to present these images in repetition, so that one canvas might contain a hundred pictures of a Campbell's Soup can, just like looking at an inventory shelf. Here again, we see the use of the everyday object to relate art to the everyday consumer life of the viewer. It was critical that Warhol called his studio "The Factory."

In 1965, there was to be a Warhol retrospective at the Philadelphia Museum of Art, to which so many guests were expected to attend that the pieces were removed from the exhibition before the guests came in order to protect the pieces. With no works up, the gathering became an exhibition of Warhol's popularity. The exhibition demonstrates that what was important was not the art objects but

instead the idea of Warhol, the persona of the artist. It was
the concept of the artist that interested people.

Warhol's "Brillo Boxes" also have connotations of
conceptual art in their resemblance to Duchamp's
readymades. Both are considered art because of context,
their place on a pedestal in a museum. They were art because of the artists' claim they were art, or, as Kosuth
would say, because of the artists' intention. But if a work is
dependent upon its creator's claim, then could it stand on
its own as a work of art? Should not a work of art have
merits that do not rely on the artist's explanation? Is, as
Derrida said, the artist dead, or is he needed to delineate
what is art and what is not? And upon what authority?
These are the questions suggested by the everyday objects
Warhol and Duchamp introduced to the art world. These
concepts would appear inseparable from the works, and it
is this fusion of the idea with the object that ultimately led
artists to question whether an object was necessary at all.

The disdain for popular culture seen in pop art went
with the spirit of the 1950's and early 1960's in the
United States and England. The pop artists reacted against
abstract expressionism and rejected the idea of the artist as
a hero. Instead of focusing on creating monumental statements like many of their contemporaries, the pop artists
were playful. Their celebration of consumerism would set
the foundations for future artists.

Roy Lichentstein looked to old comics for subject
matter, reproducing violent and sentimental comic frames
in a mechanic manner. His work is largely concerned with
style, but also suggests the speed of modern life's progression by choosing to use out of date comics as subjects. He
later applied his techniques of mechanical reproduction to
depict Picasso's and other works from art history, com-
menting on the loss of works' auras through reproduction
with an investigative quality that would appear in conceptual art. Pop art used a visual language to appeal to the
minds of the audience and asked them to question the
consumer society that surrounded them. It reacted against
art as a special commodity in a way similar to conceptual
art.

As Oldenberg escaped the museum with his store, Ed
Ruscha did so with his books. He developed unpersonal,
documentary style photographs in books and published

them. The photographs were not the works of art; they were about seeing, the everyday act being suggested in their boredom. They were like minimalist photographs. This use of the camera to document an event to be contemplated was another technique employed by the conceptual artists.

The two movements which most influenced conceptual artists, and from which most conceptual artists evolved, and which were most current with conceptual art were minimalism and fluxus. The two were opposites, reacting against one another, contemporary with one another, and both developed from the same ideas of La Monte Young. When, in 1958 Young brought a new musical composition to his teacher, his teacher had it performed to show Young how bad it was. The piece consisted of a single note played on the viola, one on the cello, and one on the violin. The piece's starkness and minimalism questioned what music was and rejected the tradition of Western music. Young later discovered the works of Cage, and like Cage began to incorporate the audience into his pieces. He began writing compositions that could not be played, and claimed himself the first conceptualist.[37] Young also began to create a compendium of various artists who reduced their medium to the extreme. With the help of George Maciunas, Young published *An Anthology* in 1963 and organized those involved into the group that would be called fluxus.

Fluxus looked back to dada for inspiration and tried to create another wave of revolutionary art, but their events usually had little straightforward revolutionary content like dada, mostly consisting of playing and flaunting eccentricity. It is ironic that though most of the events were about freedom, like the happenings before them, most events were planned and consisted of Maciunas instructing others what to do.

Other events had more thought behind them. The Czechoslovakian Milan Krizak, in an effort to open people's eyes to what happened around them, created environments on the street and persuaded people to involve themselves in them. Some, like Duchamp, said that fluxus was breaking with tradition, as dada had done, that it was

---

[37] Godfrey, Tony, *Conceptual Art*, London, 1998, 101.

healthy but could not be done again.[38] Robert Morris was a member of fluxus, but he became frustrated with the hierarchy which Maciunas and Young imposed and so removed his work from the anthology of fluxus work that Young was creating. Morris described fluxus performances as a form of vaudeville and a poor imitation of dada. Young, too, would leave the movement in frustration.

But fluxus further opened the question of what art could be. It broadened the playing field that would allow conceptual art to gain in popularity. Having accepted that art could be more than painting or sculpture, people would be more receptive to the shift away from the art object to the idea. And as fluxus had been an international movement, it prepped the world art scene for what was to come. The mainstays of fluxus were George Maciunas as the leader, Alison Knowles, Dick Higgins, Joseph Beuys, and Yoko Ono, but the group was in general fluid, with many coming and going.

Henry Flynt, associated with the fluxus movement, was the first to use the term concept art in his essay for Young's *An Anthology*. He saw concept art as being directly linked with mathematics, science, and music. He wrote, "Concept art is a kind of art of which the material is language."[39] But though he developed a theory of concept art, he practiced it little. One of his few word pieces from 1961 reads, "Concept Art: Work such that no one knows what is going on. One just has to guess whether this work exists and if it does, what it is like."[40] His language pieces, like this one, were typically paradoxical in theme, utilizing the concept as a material like a composer uses sound.

The same principles in Young's early work that inspired fluxus are similar to ideas from which minimalism developed. As the artists in Young's *An Anthology* were interested in reduction, minimalists were interested in reducing sculpture to its purest statement: the object. Minimalism as a movement consists of Carle Andre, Dan Flav-

---

[38] Ibid., 106.

[39] Flynt, Henry, "Concept Art," *An Anthology*, 1962.

[40] Godfrey, Tony, *Conceptual Art*, London, 1998, 102.

in, Donald Judd, Sol LeWitt, and Robert Morris among others.[41] And though these artists were influenced in similar ways by the industrial sculpture of David Smith, they mostly operated independently of each other. What unites their work is an effort to avoid complexity, over-refinement, and fussiness.[42] They used "industrial materials, modular units, regular or symmetrical or gridded arrangements, a kind of directness in the use and presentation of materials, and absence of craft or ornamental composition."[43] Like Reinhardt, these artists removed everything that was not art leaving clean, machined, geometric objects. These works questioned what was essential to the art object. The next step was for conceptual art to ask why is this object necessary and what makes it art.

Carl Andre created sculptures by stacking firebricks. Flavin mounted florescent lights in geometric arrangements. These works could be seen as assisted readymades, but there is always a design element that gives them the feeling of being made rather than found. In these cases, the object is important, but the arrangement of the object is what makes it function as an art object. Buying a work by Flavin was not buying a group of florescent lights, but instead the art buyer was subsidizing Flavin as an artist by purchasing his design. The mental effort, the idea, is integral, and so these minimalist pieces have aspects of conceptual art within them.

It is important to realize that works can be different levels of conceptual. Sol LeWitt's work during this time was also both minimal and conceptual in that his starting concept was a text.[44] This text was given to his assistants to perform, as a sculptor would give instructions to a foundry for a large piece. With artists becoming less involved with the physical production process, it was conceptual art that questioned if physical production was necessary.

Both conceptualism and minimalism make use of the apparently everyday object, as Duchamp did. The banal

---

[41] Batchelor, David, *Minimalism,* Cambridge, 1997, 7.

[42] Ibid., 68.

[43] Ibid., 13.

[44] Ibid., 48.

object was also used in pop art in the relation of the twentieth century urban experience drenched in materialism. Both minimalism and conceptualism depend on the viewer not taking the object literally despite there being no attempt in the works to disguise the literalness of the materials. For the critic Michael Fried there was no distinction to be made between 3D work and the readymade, nothing to transcend the literal to the pictorial.[45] What was important was the ability to recognize that an Andre or a Flavin, that a Duchamp or a Bruce Nauman could at the same time be literal and pictorial. The result from the acknowledgement of the pictorial is a moment of detachment from the real world. The result of the acknowledgement of a work's literalness makes the viewer aware of his presence, that of the object, and the space they fill. The ability for a piece to contain both of these experiences enhances its complexity beyond the physicality of the object, so that the work has a separate component, the conceptual component. To a degree, every work has this component, and the more the conceptual component is emphasized in comparison to the physical component, the more the work is a conceptual art work. Minimalist works' ability to be at the same time both simple objects and indicators of theoretical issues demonstrates their possession of the conceptual component without other elements to detract from it. Its possession of this component is what makes minimalist art to a large extent conceptual.

Because art was fashionable in the sixties it was prone to change, which also meant that critics could prescribe many new "-isms," and the audience was always hungry for the next new art fad. The 1966 minimalist exhibit *Primary Structures* drew great attention with its strong versions of formalist abstractions. Godfrey called the works "visual presentations of ideas, an activity were more conceptual than aesthetic."[46] These works were unconsciously laying the ground for something that would go further. Mel Bochner has said on multiple occasions that the minimalists believed art was unreal, contrived, and this marked the end of the Renaissance idea of art. The artists were try-

---

[45] Ibid., 65.

[46] Godfrey, Tony, *Conceptual Art*, London, 1998, 110.

ing for something different, reductive, and simple, yet they continued making objects. The objects' ordinary, industrial materials forced the viewer to decide if the works were literal or artistic, or accept the works as both. Their pure objectivity made the viewer question them. In 1988, Dan Graham noted that minimalism disillusioned the intellectual, while conceptualism was heavy handed in its morality and puritan qualities. Minimalism was subtle conceptual art.

These minimal artists would belong to the first generation of New York artists to graduate from a university. This generation afterward felt the need to destroy the formalism that the academies had institutionalized as the authoritative force. In Freudian terms, they felt the need to kill the father that kept them from their mother art. Because of their education, their theory and essays would be more complex then what had come before, often taking on the role of the art critic. Some conceptualists, such as Dan Graham, would become first known as a critic rather than as a artist.

Fried said in 1964, "something like a dialectic of modernism has in effect been at work in the visual arts for roughly a century now."[47] Modernism has been defined by its self-critical aspects, and it is conceptual art that saw an end to modernism and the beginning of postmodernism. Conceptual art made the analyzing of art not only its subject, but also its material and essence. It was the culmination of the self-critical aspects that had been evolving in modernism since before the turn of the century.

---

[47] Fried, Michael, from *Three American Painters* (1965), in Harrison and Wood, *Art in Theory: 1900-1990*, 1998, 772

4. Conceptual Art in America

Conceptualism in the United States is normally defined as beginning in the mid-sixties when conceptual art "broke decisively from the historical dependence of art on the physical form."[48] However, as the past section suggests, the conceptualists of the sixties did not make a decisive break, but instead followed neatly in the footsteps of those who came before them. Degrees of conceptual art have been practiced by various artists continually since Duchamp's readymades, and it was these artists that the conceptualists were influenced by when creating their work. So, instead of being defined by a break from the norm, this paper defines conceptualism as the period in which conceptual art was a dominant art trend.

In examining fluxus and minimalism, this text has focused on the art scene in New York. It is important to keep in mind other events that would build a foundation for the conceptualist phenomenon. Guy Debord' film *Hurdements en faveur de Sade* consisted of eight minutes of a blank screen and nonsense sound and was exhibited in the 1999 retrospective *Global Conceptualism* as a work of conceptual art. Yves Klein had an exhibition in 1958 in Paris called *Le Vide*, which consisted of an empty gallery. This was a critique, perhaps a mockery, of Debord. Cage's *4'33"* hinges on the listener knowing the concept behind

---

[48] *Global Conceptualism: Points of Origin, 1950's-1980's*, exh. cat., ed. Philomena Mariani, Queens Museum of Art, New York, 1999, VIII.

it. It is debatable whether these works are minimal or conceptual, but they contain elements of both. And the artists that produced these works were not only precursors to conceptualism, but would also work concurrently with it.

Other events outside the art world would occur contemporarily with conceptualism. Most art historians do not discuss the social climate of the sixties in their analysis of conceptualism, and most conceptualists do not make overt references to social conflict. Though artists like Kosuth denied that works of art had to relate to the external world, this does not mean the artists themselves were divorced from it, especially in the social upheaval of the sixties. There was a revolutionary tone to the conceptualist's works, "tempered by despair over the conduct of American politics (Vietnam, Watergate etc.), and energized by the insurgency and success of the Women's Movement."[49] Lippard notes, "it was no coincidence that Conceptual Art appeared at the height of the social movements of the late 1960's nor that the artists were sympathetic towards those movements."[50] More recently, Robert Morris, Hans Haacke, Adrian Piper, Yvonne Rainer, and Mary Kelly have acknowledged how issues of American politics, race, gender, and sexuality influenced their works from 1965 onwards.[51]

The space race, racial tensions, the Vietnam Conflict, protests, and assassinations would fill the period during which conceptualism would flourish, and conceptual art's rise in popularity owes a lot to this social climate. It was a time of great changes, with many people open to radical ideas and many reacting against them. In 1964, the Civil Rights Act was passed despite rioting over school integration. The country vehemently argued over the US's official participation in the Vietnam War, fueled by the omnipresence of the war's horror on television. Radical feelings would lead to demonstrations as 25,000 marched on Washington in protest of Vietnam. Civil rights would be demanded by 3,200 who walked the Freedom March from

---

[49] Pincus-Witten, Robert, *Postminimalism,* New York, 1977, 14.

[50] Lippard, Lucy, *The Pink Glass Swan*, New York, 1995, 121.

[51] Berger, Maurice, *Minimal Politics,* New York, 1997.

Selma to Montgomery, Alabama, and 4,000 would be arrested over the five day riots that burned Watts California. In 1965, Malcolm X was assassinated and three years later Rev. Martin Luther King and Robert Kennedy would be assassinated.

Race riots continued in 1967 and 1968. Bras were being burned by feminists and Neil Armstrong was the first man to walk on the moon, keeping the US's libido safe from threats of the USSR. The Vietnam War continued to cause people to question their government and the companies profiting from the war. At the same time, artists questioned the art establishment and the audiences were questioning the genuineness of the artists, in part because of their use of new and unusual methods. As mass media swept across America, its techniques also infiltrated the circles of the art world and impacted the development of conceptual art. Artists began to use video cameras, Xerox machines, and other technologies newly available to document ideas.

America was in turmoil, and it does not seem unreasonable to assume that this climate would have some impact upon artists and art audiences. As Vietnam protests continued, it seems likely that conceptual art, which rejected the galleries and museums run by those industrialists who profited from the war, would sound appealing.[52] Indeed, conceptualists were involved in anti-war projects. Mel Bochner and Robert Morris were involved in the Art Workers Coalition through the New York Art Strike of 1970 and through the creation of posters protesting the My Lai Massacre. These posters are examples of how artists were concerned with contemporary issues. If a public knew conceptualists were concerned with the same issues with which it was concerned, it is possible it would have supported these artists. Though it is difficult to establish a direct correlation between the politics of the concep-

---

[52] As Tony Godfrey states, the Museum of Modern Art "was the place to protest , because the men who sat on the museum board of trustees were the very same men who owned those huge American companies that were providing the machinery of war – and benefiting financially from it." Godfrey, Tony, *Conceptual Art*, London, 1998, 242.

tualists and the politics of the public, the revolutionary quality of both suggests a connection.

By 1973, the US had stopped bombing Cambodia, had left Vietnam, and the president had been accused of the Watergate scandal. This was the time of conceptualism's decline. Nixon resigned, 6.5 million Vietnam vets returned to mixed feelings in the states, the country was in an official recession, and there was an oil shortage. It is entirely possible that these events took the energy out of the public's desire for the art that was now as institutional as the art scene it had originally attacked. While these events may not have any direct correlation to the events in conceptualism's rise and fall, it certainly would have affected the climate of the society in which these works were created and viewed. Also, the political upheaval may have influenced the conceptualist's desire to give their work a more political aim in the seventies, as seen in the work of Hans Haacke, Sherrie Levine, Antonio Munlaer, and Joseph Beuys. These artists would create works radically different from the detached and introspective text works of Joseph Kosuth at the beginning of conceptualism.

Joseph Kosuth

The American born artist Joseph Kosuth proclaimed himself the founder of conceptual art. He created his first conceptual work, *One and Three Chairs*, in 1965. The work consisted of a photograph of a chair mounted on a wall next to an enlarged dictionary definition of the word chair, and on the floor in front of these was an actual chair. The work was designed to illuminate issues in semiology. Kosuth thought that people would only take him seriously if he was in a movement, so he tried to convert all of the painters in New York to conceptual art. In 1967, he had his first solo exhibition at the Museum of Normal Art in New York. After this, he began lecturing at the School of Visual Arts as well as acting as the American editor for *Art-Language*, a British magazine published by the conceptualist group Art and Language. His lecturing and writing have been greatly influenced by Reinhardt's definition of the tautological nature of art and Reinhardt's belief that the total activities of the artist give art works a cultural life. Kosuth would constantly tell his audience what his works meant, denying them a personal interpretation. This was crucial, as he saw meaning as his material, not form or color. Throughout conceptualism's popularity, Kosuth was one of the best known word-based artists, and through his writings, his collaborations with groups like Art and Language, and his constant output, he did more than any other artist to further conceptual art's recognition. His position in late modern art is as a teacher whose support of intellectual art over aesthetic art has been relentless.

In his 1969 essay "Art After Philosophy," Joseph Kosuth questioned whether an artist could be anything other than a sculptor or a painter.[53] He desired to separate art from aesthetics and to follow Duchamp's example in questioning the function of art. He believed that the value of the artist was determined by how much he questioned art's nature. Kosuth often cited Malevich, who believed

---

[53] Kosuth, Joseph, "Art After Philosophy I, II, III," *Studio International*, CLXXVIII, Oct., Nov., Dec. 1969.

artists should use logic and theory to create progressive work.[54] He saw artists as needing to question the language of art as a whole, and defined conceptual art by its ability to do so. His definition gave precedence to the text, allowing art to be purely conceptual. To him, the twentieth century marked "the end of philosophy and the beginning of art."[55] Since Duchamp's readymades, art had become dependent on being presented in an artistic context, such as a museum, and on its claim as art by the artist. Though influenced by Duchamp's ideas of art serving the mind, Kosuth challenged these dependencies modernism had forced upon itself. He envisioned a new art world where artists had to cultivate conceptual implications of their work and argue their explications. However, he has been criticized for his idea that art never need look outside the art world. In this, he perpetuated the modernist idea that art existed for art's sake.

In 1975, Kosuth's "Artist as Anthropologist" called for a social awareness in art. Conceptual art could no longer be solely introspective and autonomous from the outside world.[56] Kosuth's earlier work had been modern art based on a scientific model, used to examine the internal workings of art and make them explicit. His work always assigned the artist a social responsibility, but in his later work, this responsibility was redefined to examine the society around the artist. Over the coarse of conceptualism's popularity, his idea of his work's purpose has changed greatly, from being completely introspective to social commentary.

Much of Kosuth's early work utilized the photostat, a photo enlargement process, to depict definitions of terms in white on a black canvas, and the reductive qualities of these works are comparable to those of Reinhardt. Kosuth's photostat pieces are devoid of visual nicities, con-

---

[54] He, as many artists of the late 1960s, was affected by *The Great Experiment,* Camilla Gray's book on Malevich and Rodchenko.

[55] Kosuth, Joseph, *Art After Philosophy and After*, Cambridge, MA, 1991, XXIV.

[56] Kosuth, Joseph, "Artist as Anthopologist," *Art After Philosophy and After*, Cambridge, MA, 1991.

veying information as clearly as possible using text. Yet through his choice of defining words like "art" and "meaning," the works become self-referential and the viewer is caught in layers of meaning despite the works' visual simplicity. He discriminated between the art (idea), and the documentation (photostat). He did not want people to think he saw the photostat as the artwork, so he subtitled many of his works "Art as Idea as Idea," remarking on art's circular and repetitive nature. The photostat was not the actual art, so it could be trashed and remade. When critics in the late sixties began to criticize his photostat works for their similarity to canvas paintings such as those by formalist artists, he stopped doing them and began painting texts directly onto gallery walls in a similar fashion to Lawrence Weiner, another contemporary conceptualist. This would evolve through several formats of wall text, from the very straightforward, to the more designed oriented, to entire walls of crossed out text.

Kosuth was vital in leading and defining conceptual art. His work took up the questions Duchamp had voiced and reinterpreted them in terms of Reinhardt's minimal strategies.[57] However, the writings and works of Sol Lewitt were also crucial, establishing a foundation in the art world for Kosuth's, and other conceptualists', discourse.

---

[57] Bird, Jon and Michael Newman, *Rewriting Conceptual Art*, London, 1999, 56.

Sol LeWitt

Sol LeWitt began his career as a graphic artist for the architect I. M. Pei. In 1963 and 1964, he created his first sculptures, influenced by the Bauhaus and De Stijl, as a reaction to the last stages of abstract expressionism.[58] By 1965, he was creating sculptures based on open cube modules. These works looked visually complicated, but could be understood if the viewer understood the basic module that LeWitt called the works' "grammar." The term grammar was an allusion to structuralism, a critical theory that looked at the underlying structure of a text and how its parts operated.[59] He published his "Paragraphs on Conceptual Art" in 1967, followed two years later by his "Sentences on Conceptual Art."[60] These two works were important in defining conceptual art as art in which the idea is the most important aspect of the work, making the execution "perfunctory."[61] "The idea becomes a machine that makes the art."[62] He was not aiming to make beauty (though many of his works are visually interesting), but was instead cataloguing the outcome of a premise in his creation of objects. He believed that if a thing existed only as an idea, it was not a complete idea.[63] LeWitt applied minimalist logic to his work but without the interest in the literal object. As Jonathan Fineberg said, by the "late six-

---

[58] Stapen, Nancy, "Sol LeWitt," *Artnews*, XCIV, Jan. 1995, 168.

[59] Fineberg, Jonathan, *Art Since 1940: Strategies of Being*, Upper Saddle River, 1995, 306.

[60] LeWitt, Sol, "Paragraphs on Conceptual Art," *Artforum,* V, Sum. 1967, 79-83. LeWitt, Sol, "Sentences on Conceptual Art" *Art-Language,* I, May 1969.

[61] LeWitt, Sol, "Paragraphs on Conceptual Art" in Harrison and Wood, *Art in Theory: 1900-1990*, 834.

[62] Ibid.

[63] Godfrey, Tony, *Conceptual Art*, London, 1998, 152.

ties he had reasoned his way beyond the object into conceptual art."[64]

LeWitt began creating wall drawings in 1968. These pieces were executed directly on a wall so that they could not be moved. These drawings were created by a team of assistants obeying LeWitt's written instructions. LeWitt loves music and there are similarities between his written instructions and a musical score written for musicians to carry out. His hands often did not touch the drawings. This creates a distance between the artist and the physical production which questions what it means to create a work. And like Duchamp, LeWitt sought to engage the mind rather than the eye. The drawings were simple mathematical ideas worked out, parameters which were followed repeatedly until all solutions were exhausted. The process of finding all possible permutations of an idea interested him as much as the thinking.

Sol LeWitt is a particularly interesting example of a conceptualist because he has been able to combine conceptual art with a pleasing aesthetic despite this aesthetic not being one of his goals. His allowing his works to be pretty, where other conceptualists have opted for the banal to avoid distraction from the central idea, may be the main reason he still practices his form of conceptual art as he has been successful selling works. Many conceptualists during the 1960's shunned the traps of aesthetics, holding the Duchampian desire not to appeal to the eye, but to the mind. Lawrence Weiner is one example of such an artist.

---

[64] Fineberg, Jonathan, *Art Since 1940: Strategies of Being*, Upper Saddle River, 1995, 306.

Lawrence Weiner

In the early sixties, Lawrence Weiner was painting and beginning to make earthworks, creating craters with explosions. These were anti-form works reacting against the formalism of the fifties and through these works Weiner was already moving towards what Lucy Lippard would later call the dematerialization of the object. Through these works he realized his desire to "spend the rest of my existence dealing with the general idea of materials rather than the specific."[65]

In 1965, Weiner discovered that the ideas did not have to be realized; the mere written instructions were sufficient. He gave up painting for language-based art, declaring his statements to be sculpture. Weiner began to write short specific statements such as, "A field cratered by structural simultaneous TNT explosions," or, "One standard dye marker thrown into the sea." He wrote these statements with the intention of selling these ideas as works to be realized by others. However, he believed that people did not have to buy his art to have it; they could have it by knowing it. "Anyone making a reproduction of my art is making art just as valid as art as if I had made it."[66] In 1968, Seth Siegelaub held an exhibition of twenty-eight phrases Weiner had produced at a gallery in New York. The statements were published one per page in a book titled *Statements.* Some of the statements shown were for sale; others had already been realized by Weiner. Art for Weiner had evolved from the making of objects to the relationship between humans and objects. This relationship was communicated in the statements he produced. In the beginning, it did not matter how these statements were delivered: they could be spoken, they could be handwritten on a napkin, they could be typed in a book, they could be lettered on a wall. However, the presentation of the statements would gradually take on more meaning to Weiner.

---

[65] Godfrey, Tony, *Conceptual Art*, London, 1998, 165.

[66] Meyer, Ursula, *Conceptual Art, New York, 1972,* 217-218.

As with his earlier work, it was important that his word works escaped formalism by allowing anyone to understand them. He avoided use of the complex language of formalism in order to avoid alienating viewers. There was no specific audience, anyone could read the works or perform the acts. He remarked in October of 1969, "I don't mind objects, but I don't care to make them."[67]

Both Weiner and Kosuth were aware of language's dependence on context. They both used texts to show how language's meaning was dependent on place. Kosuth, for example, placed the same text on several different billboards in different cities.[68] It was a kind of deconstruction of advertising. For Weiner, the use of language was important because of the signifier/signified relationship. The signified operates in a state of continual equivalence, so it is always in search of meaning, while the signifier always works on several levels at the same time. The two are dependent upon each other without any direct correlation. Context was what established a relationship between the signifier and the signified. These aspects were received and assessed by the viewer, and it was this receivership, whether in a reader or a gallery visitor, that interested Weiner.

In 1969, Weiner was involved in the ground breaking exhibition by the art dealer Seth Siegelaub, *The January Show,* in New York, as well as the *Konzaption/Conception* show at the Stadtisches Museum. Within two years, he, Kosuth, Robert Barry, and Doug Huebler would be represented by Leo Castelli. Weiner was showing in galleries, museums, books, and catalogs. While he was represented by a major dealer and was being shown in important galleries, the art objects he produced, his statement books, remained relatively low in price in comparison to objects other artists produced. Later, when Jasper Johns' *False Start* was sold for $17 million in November of 1988, Weiner's books could still be had for $1.95.

Through the seventies, Weiner stopped using the language of hoi polloi and began to take on ideas that required more sophisticated terminology. In addition to his instructions of acts, he began to analyze art in statements

---

[67] Ibid., 217.

[68] Meyer, Ursula, *Conceptual Art*, New York, 1972, 18.

such as "Art represents a reality concerning the relationship between the potential and capabilities of an object."[69] He described art's relation to society as a service industry and felt the need for explanations to be part of the production concept of art. He explained that he chose the concept as his medium because content gives the perceptions and observations of the artist. His later pieces were more educational than the earlier instructive ones. Some would later be published as works in magazines, as well as in books and films. The presentation was becoming more of a concern for Weiner; his gallery installations of statements were stenciled onto walls in a presentation style that echoed Kosuth. In 1982, Weiner and Kosuth would be given places of primary importance in the *Documenta 7* exhibition in Germany, being seen as the most pure and logical spawn of the simplification of art concerns.[70] Ironically, critics continually praised his language-based works that explained themselves and therefore did not need a critic.

---

[69] Weiner, Lawrence, "Notes from Art," *Art Journal*, XLII, Sum. 1982,122.

[70] Frackman, Noel, "Documenta 7," *Arts Magazine*, LVII, Oct. 1982, 94.

Dan Graham

Dan Graham's first conceptual works were self-referential word pieces like Weiner's, though Graham's stem
from his career as a writer for art magazines. In 1964, Graham became manager of the John Daniels Gallery on 68th
street in New York. The gallery was showing then lesser
known artists like Lewitt, Judd, Smithson, Flavin, Andre,
and other minimalists. These artists were reconsidering the
nature of art after expressionism and pop, questioning the
institution, and they influenced Graham's writing. In
1965, he published a photo essay, "Homes for America,"
in *Arts Magazine*. This is considered to be his first major
work.[71] Many critics see him as being best known as a pho-
to-journalist.[72] Provocative writers like Graham increased
the use of language in the visual arts, exploring the nature
of representation in ocular and verbal forms. They were
signaling what would be the dematerialization of the art
object.

"Homes for America" investigated the tract housing
developments that existed everywhere and were built as
cheaply as possible without evident concern for contemporary standards of tasteful architecture. The work
demonstrated how mass production negates a genuine feeling of ownership. The work consisted of several pages of
text with accompanying photographs, showing trends in
the serial nature of the housing projects. Graham had begun to scientifically examine everyday life and how it is often defined by consumer culture. However, Graham was
using his essays to make money, taking the fee *Arts
Magazine* paid him for "Homes" and other articles and using this money to fund other art projects. In this way,
Graham was able to create art works that he did not have
to sell. From "Homes for America," Graham's work took

---

[71] Graham, Dan, "Homes of America," *Arts Magazine,* XXXIX,
Mar. 1967.

[72] "Dan Graham at John Gibson," *Arts Magazine,* XLV, Feb.
1971, 58.

on themes of mass consumption in American society. His work *Figurative* consisted of an ad placed in *Harper's Bazaar* where he printed a cashier's receipt, simply composed of a series of prices for items paid. This called attention to how context shapes a viewer's response to raw information, and in the different ways information travels in consumer society. The list of numbers printed would be easily recognizable as a receipt to any consumer due to their layout. However, printed in a different format, they would not be recognized as such. By displaying the receipt in a magazine, he suggested that the receipt offered information about the purchase and the purchaser, as any article in a magazine offers information. Recently, he described his printed works like *Figurative* as containing a utopian desire to avoid being commodified by circumventing the gallery system.[73]

If Graham's early works were concerned with the routines of everyday life and mass culture, his later works explored the complex setting these phenomena took place in. In the mid-seventies, his writing investigated how over abundance, consumerism, and leisure time grew in post-war culture. He was particularly interested in the emergence of a visible mass culture and the formation of youth cultures as independent consumer groups. He wrote on the development of punk rock in the late seventies, exploring class and gender relations. To him, punk culture was a revolt of the working class against the repression of late capitalism. However, it was not the factory workers that rebelled, but the youth, the most easily manipulated consumer class. In this, Graham saw liberating aspects of popular culture. He opposed the theories of the cultural critics Theodor Adorno and Max Horkheimer that mass culture had to oppress and exploit. Instead, it was possible for individuals to disrupt the cultural field. He believed in the optimism of Walter Benjamin, another cultural critic, envisioning a utopian postmodern culture containing hope and pleasure. Where Benjamin desired to describe the new experience born in the emergent consumer culture of nineteenth-century Paris, Graham wanted to describe the restructuring of everyday life under the phantasmagoric re-

---

[73] Graham, Dan, Lecture, University of Southern Maine, Portland, Nov. 18, 1999.

gime of twentieth-century consumerism. Throughout his conceptual work, Graham tried to reveal how everyday life has been restructured around consumerism. He hoped to break the zombie-state induced by consumer culture.

In the mid-eighties, Graham inspected links in popular culture and looked at public spaces as sites of social interactions. He wrote on architecture and the decline of the urban public space. His work throughout the nineties has continued somewhat in this vein, though moving away from the textual. Recent exhibitions have contained models made of two-way mirrors meant to demonstrate performer-audience-control relationships. This combines his interest in public spaces with performance and installation pieces he did in the early seventies, such as *Two Consciousness Projection(s)* and *Intention Intentionality Sequence.* These works are performance pieces in which the audience and a performer simultaneously view and describe each other. Each receives the description and reacts to it, revealing a cause-effect relationship in which both control the other. These pieces would later lead to video installations and mirror installations where viewing a work also meant becoming a performer. These pieces made the participant aware of how humans interact with each other and the pressure conveyed simply by being looked upon. Graham would explore this theme continuously in his works that bridged the gap between sculpture and architecture. These are a series of pavilions constructed with two-way mirrors, created for site-specific installations. The walls of two-way mirrors create an uncomfortable tension amongst the viewers since to look at the piece often means to look through the piece at someone else. Today, Graham continues this series which he began in the mid-seventies, creating functioning pavilions as well as unexecutable plans and models. Dealing with themes of social constructions and alienation, these pieces, as most all of Graham's work, demonstrate an interest in how society operates, its members communicate, and the internal structure of everyday activities.

Mel Bochner

Mel Bochner came to New York in 1964 after two years of traveling around the country. He was painting at the time in a minimalist manner, reacting against illusionism. His notebooks show he was looking at Rauschenberg and Johns, his work being driven by language and an interest in objects functioning as language.[74] He worked as an assistant to Robert Motherwell and taught art history for a time at the School of Visual Arts in New York. He describes this part of his career as working through minimalism.[75] His tiny New York apartment only allowed for small-scale drawing, and it was here, between 1965-66, that his first conceptual works began to appear. He was reading and drawing in notebooks, mostly because he could not afford materials. Necessity would play a role in his work taking on a conceptual slant, similar to the work of Ed Kienholz, who, when he could no longer afford to create his large scale environments, began to simply sell the concepts. Bochner saw drawing as immediate and being the closest thing to writing. He drew geometric diagrams that became simpler until he could envision them in his head. It was here that the object became unnecessary in Bochner's work.

In the summer of 1966, Bochner wrote a review of the *Primary Structures* exhibit, which he describes as trying to make the non-visual (mathematics) concrete. This idea would inform most of his later work. Judd and Morris's emphasis on systems and experience would become paramount in Bochner's work. He was part of the new phenomenology, recognizing art was no different from any other form of cognitive endeavor (like science) and that language was central to all representations of the world, in-

---

[74] Field, Richard S., *Mel Bochner: Thought Made Visible 1966-1973*, exh. cat., Yale University Art Gallery, New Haven, 1995, 4.

[75] Ibid., 7.

cluding art.[76] Through his minimalist work, Bochner developed a notation system of numbers that would propel his work. For a while he did wall drawings in non-durable material, emphasizing the idea more than the physical structure, as the idea would last longer. Set theory became visible in his work, as he became increasingly interested in the tension between visual and intellectual structures. His fascination with the simplicity and pervasiveness of number systems led him to create works revolving around Fibonacci's numbers and Cantor's paradox.[77] At the end of 1966, Bochner began photographing his ideas of systems using a set of wooden blocks as models. At the same time, he curated the exhibit *Working Drawings and Other Visible Things on Paper Not Necessarily Meant to be Viewed as Art* at the School of Visual Arts in New York. This consisted of four identical books on white pedestals that each contained 100 Xerox pages of what the title suggested. Benjamin Bochloh called this a critique of commercial materialism and cited it as the first conceptual exhibition.[78]

In 1967, Bochner's works became more diverse as he produced number drawings and photographs of number series. Bochner described these things as models of something rather than models for something.[79] In his photography, he abandoned his blocks and began to investigate perspective, photographing drawings of abstract grids that he would physically mangle and photograph. By 1968, he

---

[76] Ibid., 18.

[77] Georg Cantor was a mathematician who worked out a system of *degrees of infinity* explaining how infinite sets could be contained in infinite sets. Consequently, the idea of an infinite set containing an equally large infinite set has been called Cantor's Paradox. Fibonacci developed a sequence in which each term is the sum of the two previous. As the sequence progresses, the ratio of a term to the one before it approaches the golden ratio: $(1+\sqrt{5})/2$.

[78] Buchloh, Benjamin, "Conceptual Art 1962-1969: From the Aesthetic of Administration to the Critique of the Institutions," *October*, no. 55, winter 1990, 141.

[79] Field, Richard S., *Mel Bochner: Thought Made Visible 1966-1973*, exh. cat., Yale University Art Gallery, New Haven, 1995, 28.

had worked his way through photography, resulting in his *Misunderstanding (A Theory of Photography)*. The work consisted of nine quotes on index cards about photographic theory, three of which contained quotes made up by Bochner but attributed to others, undermining the illusion in language and photography. Through photography, Bochner had tried to explore illusionism, but feeling he had exhausted this avenue he now desired to re-explore literalism using ideas he had worked on in his notebooks concerning measurements.

The emergence of measurements in Bochner's work involved a return to objective and phenomenological procedures. The most important work of this period was *Actual Size*, consisting of twelve inches marked off vertically on a wall next to which Bochner photographed his head. The resulting print contained Bochner's head before the measured marks which could not measure the head accurately as they did not exist on the same dimensional plane, and depending on the size of the print, the measurement marks did not necessarily have to be standard inches. Bochner was questioning how one can know an object's scale in a photograph. This lead to what would be Bochner's most recognizable work, the measurement pieces. These works consisted of measurements marked off on walls, floors, and various objects, such as the distance of a window to a wall, or the floor to the ceiling. Through the series, Bochner questioned what does it mean to have space measured. What is the significance of knowing the distance of a window to a wall if you are not using that measurement in reference to other measurements, such as the size of a painting to place between the window and wall? Bochner saw these works not only coming from his previous number series works using wooden blocks as a kind of measurement, but also saw them as informed by Duchamp and Johns in their investigation of the limits of numbers and measurements as language. The works measured the world in an increasingly reflexive manner and demonstrated the disparity between language, in particularly mathematics, and experience.

In 1969, Bochner exhibited his first one-man show at Heiner Friedrich's gallery, and this pushed his productivity into high gear. Before this time he had been writing to fund his work. He wrote articles for *Arts Magazine* and other publications, sometimes using these opportunities to publish conceptual works like Graham did. He continued to create his measurement pieces through 1970, during which time he began to be influenced by Wittgenstein, who attacked behaviorism, and with it, idealism. He also published an essay, "No Thought Exists Without Sustained Support," which challenged Kosuth, Weiner, and Robert Barry's language pieces.[80] In 1970, Bochner began his *Theory of Sculpture* series, in which he used pebbles as a module for counting. These works began largely as a response to Robert Morris's writings on minimalist sculpture. Bochner opposed Morris's trashing of the intellectual foundations of minimalism, and in the tradition of Duchamp, called for a greater intellectual quotient in art. He viewed the counting pieces as a further abstraction from measurement. Though Bochner generated a number of these works, he did not exhaust every permutation of the counting pieces as he had exhausted series in the past. Instead, he moved on to *Theory of Painting*, which consisted of newspapers laid out on a gallery floor to create a field on which Bochner spray painted a square and then rearranged the newspapers, deconstructing the shape. After these series of projects, Bochner went through a period of reflection. In 1971, his entry in a large conceptual exhibit at Pier 18 in New York was the statement, "I couldn't think of anything to do." This period of reflection produced a reintroduction of counting into his work in various forms. *3 Ideas + 7 Procedures* used, as many pieces did, numbers written on masking tape installed on a wall. *24 Reading Alternatives* displayed on paper twenty-four ways of writing a progression of numbers, one left to right, another right to left, etc. These ideas of counting, sequences, and series would continue in his work.

Bochner has characterized his first years as working through minimalist theory. The years 1966-1973 can be categorized as Bochner's time of working through phenomenology, as he tried "to define the world (not just art) as a summation of purely mental (if not linguistic) events."[81] Throughout his work during the period of conceptualism, Bochner explored language theory, utilizing physical

---

[80] Bochner, Mel, "No Thought Exists Without Sustained Support," *Artforum,* May 1970, 70-73.

analogies and contingencies of site to relate language to the everyday world.

[81] Field, Richard S., *Mel Bochner: Thought Made Visible 1966-1973*, exh. cat., Yale University Art Gallery, New Haven, 1995, 63.

Bruce Nauman

Like Bochner, Bruce Nauman has never been interested in making art, but rather in investigation. His work
explores what art can be, what a true artist is, and what is
an artist's role in society. Between 1964 and 1966, Nauman attended the University of California at Davis and
tried to quit painting, finding it inadequate as a medium.
However, he returned to painting, attaching steel shapes to
his canvases. He found the steel too cumbersome, so he
switched to using fiberglass. He has never ceased interest
in painting, but views it as an easy solution to art. He instead desired a material in which there was a balance
between controlling the material and letting the material
take its course. The fiberglass casting for the paintings introduced him to the dynamics of presenting the inside and
outside of a work of art, a theme prevalent in his later
work with rubber and his corridor pieces. This inside-out-
side dynamic came from his interest in the molds for the
fiberglass pieces; the creation of the molds required attention to the inside of the mold which would then become
the outside of the fiberglass casted. He was also interested
in the combination of materials. The works show an interest in the visual presentation, but more important are
the concept and identity of a work's materials. He gives his
works an unfinished look, emphasizing the process and
making of the object. This unfinished look is a reaction to
the clean finish of minimalist works. While minimalist
works presented a unified object, Nauman sought to
present an object with identifiable parts so the viewer
could understand its making.
While at Davis, Nauman had access to filming equipment that he utilized to produce his first films, which like
his sculpture, focused on process. In 1965, he also began
filming performance pieces, using his body as a material to
bend and manipulate. He continued his sculpture,
abandoning the fiberglass pieces for rubber. He admired
Robert Morris, seeing his rubber pieces to be in competi-
tion with Morris's felt pieces. Working in California he
was more isolated than artists working in New York; how-

ever, his admiration of Morris demonstrates he was in touch with what other artists were doing to an extent.

At the end of 1966, Nauman felt a need to make a specific point with his work, desiring to "examine myself and what I was doing."[82] He moved to San Francisco and rented his first studio. He knew he was an artist, but could not afford materials with which to work, so he spent time alone in his studio thinking. He did not know what to do a lot of the time, but decided that art was something that an artist made in his studio, so whatever he was doing in his studio was art. Like Bochner and Kienholz, his lack of money for materials was moving him towards conceptual art. Seeing a Man Ray retrospective freed him from needing a definite purpose and he began to load his work with content from all sources of his everyday life, including the great amount of reading he was doing of authors like Wittgenstien. He used photography because of its ease and produced a series of satirical, narrative pictures of everyday life, including *Self-portrait as a Fountain.* The images recorded common events, such as a picture of a spilled cup of coffee or, in *Self-portrait,* a picture of Nauman spitting out water. He was taking events bordering on absurd and making them more absurd by documenting them. The camera was supposed to be a dumb instrument that recorded events disinterestedly, but it could not. The camera inherently focuses on an event that the photographer picks and crops the image, leaving information out of the picture. This is a form of editing that could not be avoided, no matter how artless or documentary the photo appears. The photo removes an event from its context, and that context, though not shone, may have been vital in understanding the event. For this reason, though artists lead the public to believe that the photo showed an event and could be trusted as a full and frank portrayal, the event has been doctored in order to communicate it to the viewer.

A neon beer sign in Nauman's studio window inspired him to use neon to express assertions on the role of the artist. He then combined his interest in neon with his investigation of the body from his performance pieces. Works like *Templates of the Left Half of My Body* combine themes of mind-body dualism and the figural point of

---

[82] Godfrey, Tony, *Conceptual Art*, London, 1998, 128.

reference. The piece consists of neon tubing having been molded around his body at set intervals and then set up so that they lit up in space to outline the shape of his body at these intervals. He used neon as a tool to draw in space. He became aware of Robert Rosenquist's work with neon and was greatly influenced by him. Both artists elude single interpretation with multiple levels of opposing meanings, and both use provocative materials and symbolic analogies to set up interplay between what is man made and natural.

Bruce Nauman's investigations into the role of the artist lead to his realization that society wants artists to be normal and within society's expectations, but also wants them to be outside observers and exceeded society's norms. This realization caused Nauman to address his relationship with the public in his work by intentionally keeping information from them in works like *Dark* (1968). *Dark* consisted of a 2,500 lb. slab of steel that has the word "dark" inscribed on its bottom hidden from the viewer. He also united this idea of viewer participation with the idea of public vs. private space in his installation work. In the Nicholas Wilder Gallery, he sealed off a room and placed a video camera in it so viewers could look at the space through a monitor but could not enter it. This piece was influenced by the amount of time Nauman spent in the studio alone separated from the world. In 1970, he began the installation of a series of corridor pieces, also in the Nicholas Wilder Gallery. An example of these pieces consisted of six corridors of various sizes, one only 2" wide so that one could not even see down it. There was a camera at one end off the corridors and a monitor at the other so as one approached the monitor, their body receded in the picture. The piece developed issues of concealment, disclosure, and enclosure, as all of his corridor pieces would. These pieces would lead to another series of works using tunnels instead of corridors. Often, instead of making the whole tunnels, he would make a maquette to exhibit, as it was the general idea of the space involved that was important. This series of works continued until 1981. As with all his works, these series were executed in the most unadorned fashion, so that the action or surface would not detract from Nauman's explorations.

The tunnel series inspired another set of works that utilized a chair to communicate an idea of being trapped. The first chair piece, *South American Triangle*, consisted of three fourteen foot boards suspended from a single point in the ceiling so that they formed a triangle parallel with the floor. Suspended in the center of the triangle was the chair. The work had a menacing feel as it was suspended at eye level and the viewer had to be wary of being hit. Nauman continued the chair series through 1984, some pieces having vague feeling surrounding them like *South American Triangle*, others generating political messages about apartheid in South Africa or similar oppressive situations through their titles or the isolation of the chair from the viewer by obstructive elements. In all cases, he used simple materials to deliver the idea, avoiding monumental seriousness.

The broaching of political messages in the chair pieces was continued in a body of work started in 1985 in which Nauman returned to using neon. These works are a series of large neon signs that depict images of sex and violence in garish colors. The signs flash different pictures to overwhelm the eye. The pieces exert pressure on the viewer who is attracted and repulsed, left with powerful afterimages. In these works, Nauman is continuing an investigation into the artist/viewer relationship seen in his earlier works. He continues with this series of work today and it has helped put him on several critics' lists as one of the ten best living artists.[83]

---

[83] *Artnews,* XCVIII, Dec. 1999.

Douglas Huebler

Dougals Huebler, like Nauman, never desired to create objects, but his work took a radically different path
than Nauman through conceptualism. After serving in
World War II, Huebler worked in California as a commercial artist until 1955, when he began to teach art. By the
mid-1960's he was producing minimalist sculpture, large
cubes and other geometric forms covered in formica.
These objects were intended to be simple and unpriv-
ileged, able to involve the viewer from different angles. But
he was soon greatly influenced by Robert Smithson's
earthworks, and desired to use existing objects as earthworks through a selection process similar to Duchamp's
selection of the readymade. This was taking Smithson's
work a step further, as Smithson believed one needed to
create some kind of physical residue in real space to
provide a dialectic between the idea and the object.
Huebler saw objects already existing in real space, and so
utilized what was there. In 1968, Huebler participated in
what Lucy Lippard calls the first conceptual art show.[84]
The show, entitled *Douglas Huebler: November 1968*,
consisted of a catalog without a gallery. Huebler's pieces
consisted of site sculptures: geometric shapes drawn onto
maps representing regions in real space. One sculpture
might consist of four city blocks that were contained in a
square Huebler had drawn on a map. As he was not producing anything that was not there already, Huebler na-
ively said that his work did not exist. These site sculptures
were meant to be experienced by each individual differently, dealing with the idea of multiple points of perspective as in his earlier minimal works. This would be a theme
that would run throughout his career.
    Whether using photography, maps, or textual docu-
ments, much of what Huebler produced tried to open up
the phenomena of the works by removing the aesthetic
base which has held them together. He believes intention

---

[84] Lippard, Lucy, *Six Years: The Dematerialization of the Art
Object from 1966 to 1972*, New York, 1973, 60.

is important because if an artist does not want a work to be measured on its aesthetic qualities, then it is not fair to do so. Instead of trying to convey aesthetic beauty, Huebler used his works, like his site sculptures, to put feelings of the ongoing nature of phenomena into an art context. The works do not propose anything that is not already known, but simply draw attention to certain things. Huebler was interested in people seeing the works in original ways; we see the world in a certain way, but can refresh this view by releasing it from the models of reality we have had pressed upon us. He used language with images to instruct, changing the normal sensory experience of the everyday. In this way, Huebler meant to expand the mind, desiring his audience to view the world with all the complex levels of a work of art.

Huebler's art is documentation, communicating to the viewer what he considers to be art and providing information about it. While he encourages the multiple perspectives of viewers, there is an aspect of Huebler's work that seems controlling. He tells critics what his work is about and decrees that what he says is part of the work to avoid the work being co-opted by the critics. Like Kosuth, he tells the viewer the meaning of the work, not allowing for interpretation. This is because he sees art as information he is communicating through pieces of documentation that are simple and to the point.

Huebler's most famous words are his catalogue statement for the January exhibition, "The world is full of objects, more or less interesting; I don't wish to add any more. I prefer simply to state the existence of things in terms of time and place."[85] His site sculptures exemplify this, as well as his *Variable Pieces* series. One piece in this series consists of a project to photograph every living person on the planet in order to create the most inclusive representation of humanity.

An example of Huebler's continuous interest in simply stating "the existence of things" after the peak of conceptualism occurred in 1982. The Museum of Contemporary Art in New York asked Huebler to install art in a public place because they had no exhibition space. So instead of making an installation piece in a public park or

---

[85] Meyer, Ursula, *Conceptual Art*, New York, 1972, 137.

the like, he installed works in the local newspaper. He believed that no one thing could be art, but one thing could join another in a relationship that was art. Since it was human intelligence that forms relationships, he thought the process of conceptual art was particularly effective. Over his career, Huebler published many works in magazines and newspapers, such as cartoons in the LA Weekly. He later commented that these cartoons were social commentary like Hogarth would make, but where Hogarth would show them on a wall, Huebler placed them in the paper just like any other comic. It was traditional art shifted to a non-art site. Unlike many conceptualists, he always continued to paint and draw until his death, but he used these physical works as signifiers of the art idea, not the art itself.

Kempton Mooney

Robert Morris

While Huebler desired to make no objects, Robert Morris concerns himself primarily with the object and examining its nature. Morris began his career as a painter but felt there was no direct relationship between process and result, and, influenced by John Cage, turned to sculpture in1961, influenced by John Cage. Throughout his career, Morris would search for a method of creation honestly represented in the art object and this search would cause him to constantly seek new materials.[86] His work is greatly informed by his study of the history of sculpture, particularly his interests in Brancusi and Duchamp. Pieces like *Litanies* and *I-Box* appear similar to Duchamp's readymades, yet their references gives them a critical perspective on art history. When the purchaser of *Litanies*, architect Phillip Johnson, did not pay for the work, Morris made another work reproducing *Litanies*, with documentation of the work stating that all aesthetic qualities had been withdrawn. He was removing the aesthetic from the object, as Duchamp had done with his arbitrary choosing of the readymade.

Morris is unique in his involvement with both minimalism and fluxus. In 1962, he staged a performance in which the curtain rose to reveal a wooden column which fell after three and a half minutes. Tom Godfrey notes this differed from a typical fluxus event as "it was not funny: it was not a jape but a highly structured and serious-even boring-event."[87] Unlike most fluxus happenings, there was a focus on the object without the artist trying to titillate the crowd. The next year Morris would exhibit the wooden column, unadorned, as evidence of the happening. This is an example of his work before conceptual art became a popular phenomenon. Many of these early pieces were self-referential, and these works could be seen in their

[86] "The Artist Speaks: Robert Morris," *Art in America*, LVIII, May 1970, 104.

[87] Godfrey, Tony, *Conceptual Art*, London, 1998, 107.

self-referral to be conceptual, as are LeWitt's line drawings that obtain their title from LeWitt's instructions to his draftsmen. In both, it is the process that is important, the concept of production.

During this time, Morris also exhibited in his first one-man show *Box with the Sound of its Own Making* and *Card File. Box* was a wooden box that contained a tape recorder playing a tape of the sounds of the box's construction. *Card File* was a library card file that catalogued the abstract operations of its own construction. While Benjamin Buchloh described Bochner's exhibition of xeroxed drawings as the first conceptual exhibition, Buchloh described Morris' *Box* and *Card File* as the first true conceptual pieces due to their tautological and self-referential nature.[88] Each piece asked the viewer whether the work of art was the process or the product. During this time, Morris was also publishing his investigations into sculpture based on minimal work in *Artforum*, which would be highly influential on a younger generation of artists.

Morris was a prominent figure in the New York art scene, often meeting with other minimalists and conceptualists at Max's Kansas City Bar, participating in the Museum of Modern Art Vietnam Protest in 1970, and working with Carl Andre and Mel Bochner in the Art Workers Coalition to make anti-war posters about the My Lai Massacre. These projects demonstrate the effect of the Vietnam War on some of the conceptualists like Morris, whose work contains antiwar sentiment even in his earlier happenings and installations. Morris was one of few who were able to address political issues in his works such as *Jornada del Muerto*, an installation piece in which skeletons donning soldiers' helmets ride phallic missiles through a room decorated chaotically in black and red.

Though some of his works are categorized as conceptual, he has never believed in conceptual art, stating he has had "too much of a Christian Science upbringing to be interested at this point in mind over matter. It's a lot of European idealism all over again."[89] Instead, he describes his works as process pieces, in which he is not breaking

---

[88] Buchloh, Benjamin, "Conceptual Art 1962-1969: From the Aesthetic of Administration to the Critique of the Institutions," *October*, no. 55, winter, 1990, 107.

from tradition, but is merely involved in the evolution of art. He calls his work since 1964 an investigation of materials concerned with scale, weight, and gravity. The works ask what is art, how does the spectator experience it, and through what faculties.

---

[89] "The Artist Speaks: Robert Morris," *Art in America*, LVIII, May 1970, 105.

John Baldessari

Both Morris and John Baldessari use a great variety of materials and move away from conceptual art in their later work. Baldessari grew up the son of two European immigrants and felt he did not fit into American society. He received a B.A. in art and desired to be an artist, but decided to wait. For a year he studied art history, identifying mostly with dada and surrealist ideas, before beginning his life as an artist. He desired control and to know everything, and it was in this year that he realized he would have to settle for partial knowledge. "Everyone knows a different world and only part of it. We communicate only by chance, as nobody knows the whole, only where overlapping takes place."[90] Throughout his career, Baldessari would explore the imperfect nature of communications and individual knowledge.

In 1962, Baldessari was painting abstract works in California and receiving little recognition. At times he would be driving and notice something that would remind him of his painting, and would photograph it. He used these photographs as sources for new paintings, such as parts of billboards with lettering. He became interested in pictorial fragments around his studio and photographed bits of them under magnification. He transferred these into large aluminum cutouts to be installed on walls and floor, torn and crumpled. This installation he exhibited in 1966 and encouraged the viewer to ask when was the part a whole and the whole a part. He came to the conclusion that painting had become elite, and so he would use the language of text, magazines, illustrations, and photos. He believed people could understand these easier. This theme of accessibility would continue through his career, evident in his refusal to use the complex terminology which appeared in many conceptualists' work. Baldessari also used structuralist theory in his early work, such as his 1966 work, *Pure Beauty*. The words "pure beauty" were printed by themselves, and the reader was left to wonder what

---

[90] van Bruggen, Coosje, *John Baldessari*, New York, 1990, 11.

kind of beauty. The signifier-signified relationship was un-
certain. The work was accessible in its simplicity, but
offered complexities in its reference to critical theory.
Baldessari was also working as an art teacher at the University of California, and he began a dialogue between himself
as an artist and a teacher, questioning how he made the art
he did, and using each part of his life to inform the other.
This dialogue is present in his 1976 series *Art Lessons,* a
series of paintings that presented accepted art norms, such
as guidelines for composition, and obeyed some of these
guidelines but also deviated from others. He was exploring
and testing the conventions of everyday life, especially
conventions of viewing objects.

Inspired by pop art and Edward Ruscha, Baldessari
desired to make art out of the everyday. He saw works like
his book *Some Los Angeles Apartments,* which consisted
of documentary style photos of arbitrarily chosen apartments, not as anti-art but as the only path progressive art
could take. In 1967, he began fixing photo images to
canvases using photo-emulsion and painting descriptive
text underneath them. The images were photos he or his
friends had taken or were procured from books or
magazines. In the beginning, there was no attempt at composition in the images and the name and place of the image depicted were simply stated in text at the bottom, giving the works a repetitive nature which emphasized the
tautological nature of art. He quickly realized he could
communicate more through the juxtaposition of what the
image showed and what the text conveyed. This realization
is evident in works like *Wrong,* a black and white photograph in which Baldessari stands with a tree behind him.
The picture is composed so that Baldessari is blocking the
view of the bottom half of the tree and the tree appears to
be growing out of his head. Under the image is written the
word "wrong" to suggest this is not the accepted way to
compose a photograph. Works like *Wrong* questioned the
acceptance of traditions in art education by violating rules
of composition, as his *Art Lessons* series had done.[91]

Baldessari, living in National City, California, felt
isolated from the predominate art themes of the time and
free to do what he wanted. His work was focusing on real-

---

[91] van Bruggen, Coosje, *John Baldessari*, New York, 1990, 30.

ity, which he did not see as glamorous, good, or bad, but just ordinary. His images and texts were not decorative, but simply stated what existed. In 1968, he held his first solo show in Los Angeles near a gallery in which Joseph Kosuth was exhibiting, though at the time he was not familiar with Kosuth or any of the conceptualists. Unconscious of Bruce Nauman's showing of neon signs the year before, he used two illuminated moving message signs to display texts containing reflexive messages. He was interested in pushing traditional art with new materials and commercial devices.

The next year he traveled to New York and, through the recommendation of the art dealer Richard Bellamy, met Lawrence Weiner and other conceptualists with whom he identified and became friends. That year Kosuth would write "Art After Philosophy" in which he would refer to Baldessari's work as a cartoon of conceptual art.[92] Kosuth had an aversion to painters, citing as precedence Duchamp's expression "as stupid as a painter," and Baldessari's use of text painted on stretched canvas made him a painter, though he was not the one who applied the paint (a sign painter was hired to perform the actual task). What Kosuth did not recognize was that he and Baldessari were both inquiring into the foundations of art, though Baldessari used canvas as a link to traditional art which prohibited him from being easily pigeonholed.

By the end of 1969, Baldessari was aware of conceptualists in New York and in Europe. He was no longer painting and wanted to perform a gesture that demonstrated his freedom from a singular material medium. This manifested itself in *California Map Project Part I,* which consisted of transposing the letters labeling "California" on a map onto the earth of the actual state, documented through photographs. The work combined minimalist concerns for appearance with earthwork, linking ideas and form.[93] In 1970, he performed his *Cremation Project,* in which he burned all the paintings he had created and not sold

---

[92] Kosuth, Joseph, "Art After Philosophy III," *Studio International*, CLXXVIII, Dec. 1969, 212.

[93] Collins, James, "Pointing, Hybrids, And Romanticism: John Baldessari," *Artforum,* XI, Oct. 1973, 56.

between 1953 and 1966. The unsold paintings cluttering his studio depressed Baldessari, and he desired to close this chapter of his life. Afterward, he moved to Santa Monica and began teaching again.

In the early 1970's, Baldessari departed from conceptual art to explore photography and how photography operates. Daniela Salvioni believes this is where he has made his real contribution to American art.[94] Baldassari had realized he does not have to use words to create works that spoke to the mind rather than the eye. He does so using techniques such as pointing in pictures, using it as a nonverbal way of isolating information.[95] In a 1989 exhibit, he showed manipulated photographs to demonstrate how the act of looking operated in photographs, focussing on sexuality. His photography through the seventies and eighties has been described as becoming richer, but simpler and more ambiguous. His deadpan style is evocative on many levels, often with an emotional element such as in *Mondrian Story* a photograph depicting a pair of feet standing next to some flowers. The combination of the flowers and with the subjects inability to show his head suggests regret, however the tone is so understated that the viewer feels unsure of how to define it, making the situation seem all the more real. Baldessari's work is straightforward, sometimes humorous, but always with an element of truth below the surface.

In the early seventies, Baldessari was teaching at the California Institute of the Arts and gained access to film equipment. He began to create films that tried to analyze film the same way he had set out to understand art, taking the medium apart and putting it together again. He challenged the conventional ways a story could be told, such as in works like *Title, 1973,* which purposefully was devoid of plot in order to hinder the forward movement of the story. The work disrupts the audience 's idea of film and through it Baldessari is inventing his own vocabulary of cinema. It is an example of how throughout his work, Baldessari has been less interested in the form art takes

---

[94] Salvioni, Daniela, "Letters from France," *Arts Magazine,* LXIII, Sum. 1989, 105.

[95] Ibid., 54.

than in the meaning images provoke.[96] Not interested in supporting the progression of modern painting and sculpture, he uses a variety of media to express ideas of gathering, sorting, and recording information. His blend of humor has also been influential to many of the artists who emerged in the 1980's.[97]

------

[96] van Bruggen, Coosje, *John Baldessari*, New York, 1990, 141.

[97] Cameron, Dan, "Art and its Double," *Flash Art*, no.134, May 1987, 72. Among the artists influenced by Baldessari, Cameron lists Louise Lawler, Eric Fischl, David Salle, and Matt Mullican.

On Kawara

On Kawara, a Japanese artist who should be mentioned briefly as he moved to New York in 1965, remarked to Ursula Meyer in October of 1970 that "recreation is more important than creation."[98] Kawara was an acquaintance of Dan Graham in the mid-1960's and Graham in an interview recalled Kosuth following the two of them around in order to get ideas.[99] Kawara's work is his actual existence. Beginning in 1966, he has documented his everyday life, mailing friends, fellow artists, and critics postcards citing the time he woke up that morning. In a world where more and more of life was being covered by the media, this artist turned documentation into a life's work, not without social commentary on the minute details of everyday life we find being reported to us. Kawara's use of documentation displays a general mistrust of the object for reasons such as commodification and the implication that a work could actually be finished, as his series of work will only be concluded by his death.

---

[98] Meyer, Ursula, *Conceptual Art*, New York, 1972, 38.

[99] Graham, Dan, Lecture, University of Southern Maine, Portland, Nov. 18, 1999.

Trends in Conceptual Art

Like Kawara, many conceptualists used series as an important part of their work. Artists used series and systems similar to scientists, tracing out the various permutations of an idea. LeWitt uses series to a lesser extent, establishing a set of rules and running a series until all possibilities are played out in his drawings. An extreme example is Roman Opalka, whose work since 1965 has consisted solely of painting in white on a gray background the series of numbers from one towards infinity. He speaks each number into a tape recorder and photographs himself each day. Opalka's canvas series still continues with its systemic counting and evidently will not be finished until the death of the painter. Other conceptualists, like Bochner, have abandoned their original systematic schemes for more politically minded works.

Besides serial and systematic methodology, another important tool of the conceptualists was the use of documentation. But with enough documentation, the evidence tended to glorify the idea being presented, so that with enough support, anything could seem grand and important. Many conceptualists found trying to eliminate the art object impossible; they simply could not because there was always something to be commodified. When all that was left was the documentation, the gallery would show glorified pieces of documentation. Lawrence Weiner's work is an example; he reduced his sculptures to simple statements in order for the work to be communicated. However, once these statements were written, the written texts began to be treated like an art object, being displayed in galleries.

Conceptual artists rejected galleries, producing work that was not fit for gallery showings, but galleries still showed the works that then appeared banal and bland in a gallery context. Today, galleries and museums put together retrospectives, however, these shows seem boring as they consist of hundreds pieces of documentation hung on a wall for the viewers to read. Pieces such as Huebler's *Eleven Sugar Cubes,* which appeared as four photos in *Art in America* (June, 1970), make little sense removed from the context and format for which they were intended, and which was part of the structure of the piece. If this piece were hung in a gallery, it would seem boring, for the idea was tailored for a magazine and anyone who wanted to see it could have seen it in a magazine. There would be no reason to see the work replicated for a museum, as opposed to the magazine reproduction. Yet museum curators still cling to the idea that art should be shown in museums.

One of the major supporters of conceptual art was Seth Siegelaub, who invented many of the processes for showing works of conceptual art outside the traditional gallery system. Siegelaub saw books not as signifiers for works, but as part of the work and as documentation of the work. They were important because as art became a source of information, books and catalogues took the place of exhibits. There are many examples of this, one of the most famous being the January Show. The title, which in full was *January 5- 31 1969*, described not only the length of the show's existence, but also the length of the showroom's existence, as a business was going to move into the space in February. The showroom was an office space Siegelaub had rented as a kind of reading area for the exhibition. It looked like a business waiting room, with a receptionist, Adrian Piper, whom Siegelaub had hired to answer questions. The look of the space was not important, just that it was not associated with a gallery. However, the space was located in a gallery district on East 52nd Street in New York City. All the information had been printed in the catalogue, which people came to the office space to read and discuss. Visual presentations by the four artists involved were not necessary because the primary information was represented in the catalogues. There were, however, a few physical pieces placed casually around the space, such as documentation photos sitting on a windowsill. Critics did not know how to respond to this and so few did. John Perrault wrote one of the few reviews of the exhibit in *The Village Voice*, writing that the exhibit was really the catalog, but he then went on "to concentrate on the 'supplementary materials.'"[100] He realized that these

---

[100] Perrault, John, "Art Disturbances," *The Village Voice,* Jan. 25, 1969, 14-18.

were not the real works of the exhibit, but wrote about them out of convenience, unsure how to approach the real works in the catalog.

Siegelaub was important because he was the curator as an artist. He innovated new ideas of how to represent artists. In shows like the *November Show* in 1968, a showing of Huebler's work, he restructured the exhibition as a catalogue. He repeated this restructuring in the *March 31 Show* of 1969, showing 31 artists in a catalog, one for each day of the month. He created shows in the way other conceptual artists created their works, his material being other artists' works. Similarly, Lucy Lippard's activities were indistinguishable from the activities of many artists. Critic Peter Plagens described Lippard as the true artist in her *557,087* exhibition, having given the show a total and pervasive style.[101] Lippard describes the show as an exercise in "'anti-taste' as a compendium of varied work so large that the public would have to make up its own mind about ideas to which it had not been previously exposed."[102] It was not solely a conceptual art show, since it contained conceptual art, minimal art, outdoor art, and idea art. Due to the great scale of the exhibit and Lippard's relative inexperience curating, many of the works designed or installed for the exhibit were executed incorrectly or the works were left unfinished. Despite this, Plagens noted the show would be looked back on as the "first sizable (i.e. public installation) exhibit of 'concept art.'"[103]

As mentioned in part two of this paper, there is no definition that fits all conceptual art, but rather all pieces will fit the definitions to varying degrees. However, there are trends in conceptual art, such as its lack of color. Mel Ramsden describes the idea of conceptualism having a style as a joke.[104] It was about finding alternatives for critical inquiry. However, many people were buying work for

---

[101] Plagens, Peter, Review of *557,087*, *Artforum*, VII, Nov. 1969, 64.

[102] Lippard, Lucy R., *Six Years: The Dematerialization of the Art Object from 1966 to 1972*, New York, 1973, 111.

[103] Plagens, Peter, Review of *557,087*, *Artforum*, VII, Nov. 1969, 64.

its appearance, buying into an aesthetic of conceptual art. [105] There are several reasons for the trend of bland appearing conceptual art, one being that conceptual artists were typically purists about art and the lack of color gave the works a puritan look. Another reason was that black and white provides a sort of anonymity and yet an authority that helped to convince the viewer of the validity of the idea as a work. Also, the use of color meant more money for materials, and one of the major catalysts for conceptual art was the artist's lack of funds, as seen in the career's of Bochner and Nauman. And finally, black and white has a journalistic and honest look to it; it supported the idea that the photographs and texts were not works of art, but were rather mere documentation of the work. However, there are exceptions to this generalization of conceptual art, like LeWitt, who though he began without color, introduced color into his wall paintings of the seventies.

Another important unifying aspect of conceptual art was that the artist did not concentrate on giving the works an aura, for often he had no concern for the context the work would be shown in. A work could be communicated in a newspaper, on a billboard, or in a book. This blurred the idea of the artist a little. Most pieces were presented in documentation or as primary information, i.e. a book of conceptual art was not a secondary source about the works, but expanded the works, as the reader was receiving primary information. This demonstrates how some conceptual artists avoided the production of primary objects, as texts that works were presented in could be printed by the hundreds. One never saw an original, only a single manifestation out of multiple. This put the viewer in "intellectual discomfort" and emphasized the participation of the viewer in the work by calling for an active reading. [106] The conceptual work does not simple couch a proposition, but presents information which, only after analysis, can be interpreted by the reader.

---

[104] Ramsden, Mel, "Interview," *Flash Art*, no. 143, Nov./Dec. 1988, 108.

[105] Ibid.

[106] Godfrey, Tony, *Conceptual Art*, London, 1998, 142.

There have been other themes that have run through a number of conceptual works, if not all of them. Ideas of self-reference, dematerialization, and the exploration of perceptions are common themes. Another is the literary theory of structuralism, "which posited meaning as a decipherable, universal language structure underlying the form."[107] Many conceptualists, such as Kosuth and LeWitt, prescribed to this train of thought. The ideas of Wittgenstein and Benjamin were also influential upon many conceptual artists. These trends come in part from the communication of the conceptualists with each other, despite their lack of cohesion as a real movement.

Elimination of the object was supposed to eradicate concerns with style, quality, and permanence. However, as conceptual art grew popular, there developed a "conceptual art style" that many artists tried to imitate with no understanding of the content. This look consisted of the documentary black and white photos, and the use of text as primary information. There was also a tendency in the public to look at these pieces of documentation as valuable objects in themselves, as they have been written about by major critics and hung in museums. However, this ritualization of the object misses the point, for if the concept is truly the art, then the destruction of these pieces of document should not matter.

It was not simply the gallery system to which conceptual art demonstrated a need for an alternative, but also the vocabulary of art. The traditional language of art was simply no longer adequate to describe conceptual art. Terms were invented to clarify the complex theories that developed behind the first artists to have graduated from universities. Many of the conceptualists were known for their writing as well as their artwork. LeWitt's "Sentences on Conceptual Art" and "Paragraphs on Conceptual Art" became standard reading material for younger artists.[108] These works were published in *Artforum* and *Art-Lan-*

---

[107] Fineberg, Jonathan, *Art Since 1940: Strategies of Being*, Upper Saddle River,1995, 306.

[108] LeWitt, Sol, "Paragraphs on Conceptual Art," *Artforum*, V, Sum. 1967. LeWitt, Sol, "Sentences on Conceptual Art" *Art-Language,* I, May 1969.

guage and their general acceptance demonstrates that the anti-formalist approach became as institutional as formalism.

The function of the artist and the critic has always been divided. Ursula Meyer describes the relationship in a manner similar to Greenberg: "The artist's concern was the production of the work and the critic's was its evaluation and interpretation."[109] This worked well for formalist artists, who were concerned with formal issues like color, shape, and composition and not necessarily with critical theory. But assigning evaluation as the ciritc's responsibility does not allow for a work to contain self-reflection, which has been a major tenet for many modernist movements. Many conceptual artists furthered this idea by taking on the roles of both the artist and critic through their use of critical methodologies. The conceptualists were concerned with the art world's dependence on critics, for if a critic offers an interpretation of conceptual art, and it differs from the artist's intention, it is ignoring part of the work. Huebler said, "What I say is part of the artwork. I don't look to critics to say things about my work. I tell them what it is about."[110] Conceptual art made ideas of work known when other works had hidden the idea, forcing the critic to interpret.

As many conceptualists looked at it, "all art after Duchamp is conceptual in value because art only exists conceptually."[111] Conceptualists such as Kosuth saw much of art as being called art because it resembled the traditional idea of art and was dependent on the traditional rationale of art. However, artists like Kosuth were full of contradictions, talking about pure conceptual art, but creating pieces, such as his *Information Room,* that were filled with objects. So while the investigation is the artwork, the objects are necessary for the investigation. The art is not the object, but is the artist's idea of art. Though

[109] Meyer, Ursula, *Conceptual Art*, New York, 1972, VIII.

[110] Shirey, David, "Thinkworks," *Art in America,* LVII, May/June 1969. Good. Describes works by Huebler, Barry, Kienholz, and Kosuth.

[111] Kosuth, Joseph, *Art After Philosophy and After*, Cambridge, MA, 1991.

the objects are subordinate to this idea, the idea is arguably still dependent on the object. Some artists were more able to detach themselves from the art object than others. Such an artist was Bernar Venet. Venet's art was knowledge, taking form in the documentation of science. He introduced mathematics and physics lectures to audiences of artists, and these acts of informing left no object behind. But the idea of dematerialization was not original to conceptual art. Conceptualists were acting in the tradition of Klein's *Le Vide* and Warhol's 1965 exhibition in which no works were exhibited. In both the work of the precursors and the conceptualists, there was no object produced, rather the work consisted of solely an idea.

Many critics, like Lucy Lippard, originally cited dematerialization as a prime characteristic of conceptual art. However, hindsight has pointed out what some artists, like Mel Bochner, have always believed, that "dematerialization is an inaccurate term, that a piece of paper or a photograph is as much an object, or as "material" as a ton of lead."[112] During the 1960's, Lippard held hopes that conceptual art would be able to avoid the general commercialization of the artist.[113] At the time, it seemed that no one "not even a public greedy for novelty, would actually pay money, or much of it, for a xerox sheet; ... it seemed that these artists would therefore be forcibly freed from the tyranny of a commodity status and market orientation."[114] However, within a few years, conceptual works were being sold for substantial sums by major galleries like Leo Castelli's; conceptual art had been commercialized despite its emphasis on the idea rather than the object. Dan Graham, who utilized magazines as an alternative to the gallery market, has suffered a disillusionment in a similar way to Lippard. He believes that the idea of dematerialization was naïve since artists, including himself, could not make a living without the selling of objects. Many tried to supplement their income through writing and teaching, but this became tiresome and took time and energy away from

---

[112] Lippard, Lucy R., *Six Years: The Dematerialization of the Art Object from 1966 to 1972*, New York, 1973, 5.

[113] Ibid., 263.

[114] Ibid.

their work. Yet, some minor breakthroughs were made by artists' efforts at dematerialization, such as work that was easily transported and mailed, and works that could appear in multiple places at the same time, such as magazine and catalogue works.

One of the major problems of conceptual art derived from its denouncing of quality. This made it hard to discern the significance of the work. Its attack on modernist ideas of aesthetic have been called the endgame of modernism by Ursula Meyer.[115] However, it never created a terse standard to judge against. It lacked a methodology that would hold up to its own weight, displaying document objects while claiming dematerialization.

During the late 1960's, conceptual art became the mainstream in the art world. Godfrey describes it as having become a "philosophical homeland" in the early seventies.[116] Michael Rush calls conceptualism, along with minimalism, "the dominant forms of the period. 'Unfettered by object status,' Lucy Lippard wrote, 'artists were free to let their imaginations run rampant.'"[117] But by 1973, conceptual art was losing popularity. Statements being hung on walls were losing their cutting edge. The shock had worn off of the audience; they were tired of looking at visually bland art. Though conceptual art continued to thrive in Europe and other places, in America came the return of style and materiality. The mid-seventies brought many genres to the market because if the idea could make it as a work of art, anything could. Narrative art, photo art, and appropriation art were all spin-offs of conceptual art and its predecessors. Many artists maintained the appearance of conceptual art, but lacked the content and creativeness of the 1960's. A few artists continued to keep conceptual art alive through the late seventies, but there was a shift in ideology: a reaction against theory and the reemphasis of the object to which the gallery system was more accustomed. This shaped the forms neo-conceptual works would take.

---

[115] Meyer, Ursula, *Conceptual Art*, New York, 1972, 33.

[116] Godfrey, Tony, *Conceptual Art*, London, 1998, 352.

[117] Rush, Michael, New Media in Late 20th Century Art, New York, 1999, 78.

In 1975, *The Fox*, a publication put out by the Art and Language group in America, discussed the failure of conceptual art with its institutional character of art and the limitations of art as an idea.[118] It noted that conceptual art had no sense of reality as it focused on art itself, the internal, and divorced itself from everything external.[119] In the sixties, good art was seen as outside the system of culture, but in the seventies it was realized that a work could not exist outside the system. Society began to be seen through a postmodernist perspective, as decaying powers without a common goal.[120] As there is no common goal to serve as a center of culture, no work could be seen as outside of this goal. The public was no longer seen as a homogenous group, but as demographic groups, and art could no longer be seen to target the public, but only as aimed at small groups of people. Focus shifted from the artist and art content to a focus on transmitting information and new forms of communication, without which content and meaning could not be trusted. Kosuth's days of dictating a work's meaning were over; now artists concentrated on the idea of how meaning is different for everyone. In the sixties, artists were reading Wittgenstein; now artists were reading Derrida, Barthes, and Foucault.[121]

Though many artists had tried alternatives like teaching and writing, many conceptualists had to return to the galleries in order to sell work and make money. Michael Baldwin looking back noted that conceptual art was successful as it smashed many stereotypes of what art should be, but at the same time it created a kind of iconography of administration.[122] The artist had become a businessman by using writing and teaching to "sell" his works to an

---

[118] Staniszewski, Mary Anne, "Conceptual Art," *Flash Art*, no. 143, Nov./Dec. 1988, 90.

[119] Clegg and Guttmann, "On Conceptual Art's Tradition," *Flash Art*, no. 143, Nov./Dec1988, 99.

[120] Ibid.

[121] Ramsden, Mel, "Interview," *Flash Art*, no. 143, Nov./Dec. 1988, 108.

[122] Baldwin, Michael, "Conceptual Questionaire," *Flash Art*, no. 143, Nov./Dec. 1988, 105.

audience. This would continue into the eighties, where artists intentionally commodified the art object and focussed on issues like industrial production and the difference between high culture and low culture, reading theory like Walter Benjamin, Rudolf Carnap, and Gilbert Ryle.[123]

Referred to by some as neo-conceptual art or post-conceptual, the idea-based work that appeared in the eighties had a different flavor. It repeated the images of conceptual art with another layer of meaning developing from their appropriation. Works were concerned more with political and social issues. Some replaced the document with a cynical materialism. Artists sold objects with the purpose of irony, accepting the fate determined by society in order to win at the game of art on their terms. The commodity used in neo-conceptualism admits the disappearance of the individual and shows social, economical, political, and psychoanalytic issues. Some work succeeded with a dialectical response to mass culture, but the majority of these artists disguised their lack of comment with cynicism.

---

[123] Ibid.

5. Forever After?

Kempton Mooney

Did conceptual art actually continue into the eighties and up to today, or have groups of artists just been heavily influenced by the conceptualist movement? How much of an influence did conceptual art have? I contend conceptual art continued to evolve after the decline of the actual conceptualist movement. Though it lost its popularity, it was never abandoned. Michael Newman says "not only have conceptual artists who emerged in the 1960's and 1970's continued to produce work, exerting a manifest or subterranean influence, also artists with a later formation ... have developed conceptual approaches in interesting new directions."[124] For this reason, he calls conceptual art an unfinished project. Also, some artists applied the methodologies of conceptual art to other processes, further spreading the reach of conceptual art's influence. This demonstrates that conceptual art has had a great impact upon the contemporary American art scene.

There are a number of ways to investigate the present condition of conceptual art. This last section of the paper is divided into three parts: The Conceptualists, The Critics, and The Next Generation. The first part will describe the ideas and work of the original conceptualists after the decline of conceptualism. The next part will look at how critics are writing about conceptualism today. The last part will look at the work of the neo-conceptualists and post-

[124] Newman, Michael, "An Unfinished Project?" *Kunst and Museumjournaal*, VII, 1996, 102.

conceptualists and the work of a few artists who do not fit into these categories but have nonetheless been affected by conceptualism's influence. I argue that these investigations will reveal conceptual art to have effected the way many artists create work and how many people think about art.

The Conceptualists

In his "The 1960's: Crisis and Aftermath," Ian Burn writes that from his perspective, conceptual art in the United States and England failed and that its goals had been unattainable.[125] Burn was a prominent member of the British group Art and Language. He produced published works that analyzed power relationships, commodity productions, and exchange in the art world. His later work after conceptualism's decline was a return to landscape paintings. He bought amateur landscape paintings from yard sales and other local sources and modified them, overlaying them with a sheet of plexiglass on which he printed text. Adrian Piper, one of his contemporaries in America, has written articles in response to Burn, saying that though the goals of the conceptualists were unattainable, the real value of conceptual art lay in its introduction of intellectual work in general as an artistic medium for visual artists.[126] In this way Piper argues that conceptual art, and in particular Burn's work, has been a success.

Burn defined conceptual art as a replacement of visual objects with arguments about art, as an inquiry into the nature of art, and as intending to bring about change. Conceptual art opened the door for people to stop packaging their work in visually pleasing forms and gave them the license to use anything. Bochner used math, Graham used architecture, and Venet used physics. These artists are examples of how conceptual art freed artists from being restricted to an art school mindset. Piper says, "Conceptual art taught us that artists can think about things, too, and read things, and write things, and analyze them and research them."[127] She believes conceptual art brought an end to formalism and art for art's sake as an autonomous

---

[125] Burn, Ian, "The 1960's: Crisis and Aftermath," *Writings in Art History*, North Sydney, 1991, 115.

[126] Piper, Adrian, "Ian Burn's Conceptualism," *Art in America*, LXXXV, Dec. 1997, 72.

[127] Ibid., 74.

realm independent of the world because many artists were drawing from fields previously considered off limits. However, I disagree in that it is inherent in conceptual art's nature to be focused internally, even if it looks outside art for new methods of investigating itself. This leads to a tautology in which little outside the art world is impacted, producing art for art's sake. But she makes a good point that genres such as appropriation art and mixed media were inspired by the thinking across disciplines that resulted from concentrating on ideas.

Piper compares conceptual art to Marx's economic analysis of neoclassical economics and Frege's analysis of the concept. All examine and criticize "the content, form, or practice of the discipline itself."[128] She believes conceptual art should be revered as these other works have been. Burn argued that in using mass media, he became aware of mass media's hypocritical political and economic functioning in capitalist society. Piper refutes this, noting that he was using capitalism against capitalism, fighting fire with fire. Piper continues that though conceptual art may have been generated by capitalist society, this does not mean it supported capitalism. Burn also stated that after you realize that your idea works can be sold, how can you believe you are being subversive when the works were supposed to reject commodification. But Piper answers that you can buy and sell ideas that subvert buying and selling ideas, questioning ownership. It is interesting to see that these two important figures in the heyday of conceptualism hold such differing views of its success.

Doug Huebler was more optimistic than Burn in his assessment. He believed art historians wrongly look back upon conceptual art as trying to collapse the museum and gallery institutions. This allows critics of conceptual art to describe it as co-opted because "it (necessarily) remained thoroughly within the art system."[129] If one thinks of conceptual art as battling the galleries and museums, then one judges it on how closely it "conforms to the correctness of

---

[128] Ibid.

[129] Huebler, Doug, "Saboteur or Trophy? Advance or Retreat?" *Artforum*, XX, May 1982, 72.

practice that point of view assigns to it."[130] This was inaccurate to Huebler as the idea of correctness cannot be applied to the dialogue that he saw conceptual art trying to assume. Huebler believed conceptual art did not desire to be confrontational, as head-on confrontation would have failed to produce an effective discourse, and would have rendered conceptual art a forgettable nothing. He also disagreed with Kosuth's implications that conceptual art is art as ideas, which gives critics grounds to judge conceptual art's purity by its dematerialization of the art object.

To critics like Calvin Tomkins, conceptual art was a style consisting of nothing more than the idea, reducing its status to minimalism's footnote, the final step in a century long process.[131] Tomkins saw conceptual art disappearing into philosophy, causing America to lose interest while Europe was still responsive to it. While certain aspects of this may be true for some of the more extreme conceptualists, Huebler believed conceptual art to concern itself with engendering new views of the world, which it has barely explored its potential in doing. Conceptual art is a receptacle for content generated by viewers' reconstitution of its terms, its forms, and its references to the world. Huebler believed conceptual art served this end well and was therefore successful in accomplishing its goal.

Huebler worked continually until his death in 1997. He, like Burn, had been working with superimposing text over paintings, exploring the relative accuracy of language and meanings. It is interesting to note, if one's impact on the world is relative to the size of one's obituary, that Gianni Versace, who died within a month of Huebler, had a larger obituary in the *New Art Examiner*.[132]

Bochner, as Burn and Huebler, returned to painting, though he now says he has always considered himself a painter, and that he simply stopped for a while. Bochner explains:

---

[130] Ibid.

[131] Tomkins, Calvin, "The Art World: An End to Chauvanism," *New Yorker*, LVII, Dec. 7, 1981, p. 146.

[132] "Douglas Huebler," *New Art Examiner*, XXV, Sept. 1997, 19

> I had answered to my satisfaction all the questions that I was addressing about how language and space intersect. The problem, in its original analytical terms, was exhausted. There were two choices: totally abandon the visual or see if I could renegotiate the terms of painting.[133]

Also, in my opinion, many of the conceptualists realized that after the initial shock had worn off, people did not want to view simple texts or bland documents when they desired art. They desired visual excitement and so the conceptualists tried to make their textual work or investigations more visually exciting. I think Huebler and Burn did so in a rather uninventive way, simply putting something visually stimulating behind the text to attract the viewer's eye.

LeWitt is still creating wall drawings, though he has gradually moved from his original pencil drawings of hatchmarks to instructions for geometric color paintings.[134] Some critics, like Robert Pincus-Witten, express concern that LeWitt's ideas have not progressed and that he is still "realizing older projects."[135] But his wall drawings continue to receive praise from other critics for their simplicity, beauty, and intellectually stimulating qualities "without any loss of clarity or perceptual punch."[136] Since 1977, LeWitt has been given at least 316 solo exhibits and has been displayed in more than 530 group shows.[137] At a retrospective in New York, Mary Sherman praised his

---

[133] Meyer, James, "The Gallery is a Theater," *Flash Art*, XXVII, Sum. 1994, 100.

[134] Stapen, Nancy, "Sol LeWitt," *Artnews*, XCIV, Jan. 1995, 168.

[135] Pincus-Witten, Robert, Postminimalism into Maximalism: American Art, 1966-1986, Ann Arbor, 1987, 94.

[136] Kalina, Richard, "Sol LeWitt," *Art in America*, LXXV, Nov. 1997, 122.

[137] Littlejohn, David, "On and Off the Wall," *The Wall Street Journal*, Mar. 10, 2000, W 16.

work's undermining the notion that artwork is unique.[138] However, it remains that his concepts are sold just as a painting would be. In May 1987, art dealer David McKee paid $26,400 for a LeWitt drawing at an auction. The nature of LeWitt's work meant McKee was actually buying the right to execute the idea, this being the first time an intangible piece of conceptual art was sold at auction in America.[139] The previous owner had executed the piece drawn on a wall and erased it once the concept was sold to the auction house to preserve its value as an original. The auction house had the drawing installed for the auction and had it erased afterwards for the same reason. The drawing itself, though it could be made by anyone, is moved from place to place as a unique object, similar to a traditional painting. While LeWitt has been lauded for undermining the original, he has simply shifted the function of the original away from the easily transportable. It is questionable whether LeWitt can be blamed for this as he has said that anyone can validly produce one of his works despite owning the rights to the idea or not. He has always been interested in the idea that arose in the seventies that a person did not have to be trained to produce artwork.

Kosuth's belief in the value of conceptual art is evident in his persistent production of textual works. He has been invited to produce a number of public works, one installing text on a garage in Japan by chiseling it into the brick. He has done a similar work in France, as Europe offers more venues for his work.[140] He says he is now attempting to make his work accessible not only to connoisseurs, but also to the general public. His works are still concerned with issues of language and meaning, and often contain paradoxical content, such as using a physical object to tell what is not present.

Kosuth also continues to lecture and write to support the ideas in his works. His 1996 article, "Intentions," de-

---

[138] Sherman, Mary, "Sol LeWitt," *Artnews*, XCII, Nov. 1993, 170.

[139] Small, Michael, "Talk About Lines," *People's Weekly*, XXVII, May 25, 1987, 43.

[140] Macadam, Barbara, "A Conceptual Artist's Self-Conception," *Artnews*, XCIV, Dec. 1995, 126.

scribes the return of painting in the eighties as demonstrating the emptiness of works that rely on critics to supply their meanings.[141] This is similar to his opinion of the formalist painters he reacted against in the sixties, like Kenneth Noland and Jules Olitski. He believed these artists sent works to Clement Greenberg, a popular critic, who assigned them meaning. For Kosuth, anyone could paint, what an artist had to do was think, like a physicist or a chemist, and he expected that only a select few would understand his work, as only a few might understand a chemical experiment's significance.[142] This is a view he continues to support, though his recent public works also try to reach a broader audience because of their location. For him, conceptual art rethought the responsibility of the artist. Though he believes conceptual art to be valuable, his view on the return of this hollow painting demonstrates conceptual art's failure in its goal to reclaim meaning.

Like Kosuth, Weiner is still producing word-based pieces, and is finding Europe a more receptive audience. In 1996, he was commissioned by the city of Prague to install what he called *City Project*, instructive word pieces spray painted on to street corners so that they were available to the public. Weiner, like Kosuth, has been doing a lot of public works, making installation and presentation a large part of his work. This continues his original notion of creating pieces to be perceived as extensions beyond the pictorial experience.

Baldassari's new works also look fairly similar to his work in the mid-seventies. In a 1998 exhibit, he showed works on canvas that had images on the upper portion and text on the lower portion. An example is a black and white set of lips printed on to a canvas and printed underneath the text "It had to be done."[143] Clifford described it as obscure with a dead pan wit, though she omits discussing the

---

[141] Kosuth, Joseph, "Intentions," *Art Bulletin*, LXXVIII, Sept. 1996, 409.

[142] Macadam, Barbara, "A Conceptual Artist's Self-Conception," *Artnews*, XCIV, Dec. 1995, 125.

[143] Clifford, Katie, "John Baldessari," *Artnews*, XCVII, Apr. 1998, 176.

structural issues, such as the ambiguous relationship between the text and image.

Opalka has continued his earlier work by continuing to execute his numbered paintings as if it were his duty to execute the series that will end with his death. As explained earlier, Dan Graham has continued creating works that explore the controlling relationships in society, using his pavilions as a way to demonstrate what the act of looking entails while at the same time creating objects that utilize light beautifully. Bruce Nauman, as discussed earlier, continues to use neon as well as video to convey his ideas simply and avoiding a monumental scale. These are examples of artists who have furthered the ideas that fueled their early conceptual works but have been able to fit into the commodity driven art market by creating fine objects.

The Critics

Benjamin Buchloh has been writing about conceptualism since the early seventies and has decided conceptualism failed. He sees conceptual art's primary purpose to have been to liberate the world from traditional forms of perception, however, he claims its optimistic endeavors turned it into a farce. Though it had turned up what Adorno called "the totally administered world," Buchloh says this world has been set up again.[144] Robert Pincus-Witten says something similar in that "conceptualism gave way to an unrepentant Expressionist volubility" which he has dubbed maximalism and has revived object driven works. [145] Buchloh adds that conceptual art sold out to the capitalist commodity fetishism that they tried to critique.[146] Critic Kathryn Hixson defends conceptual art, placing the blame for its commodification not on the hands of the artists, but instead on those who try to explain it. She believes that our urge to commodify conceptual art "in linear historical terms is simply a self-defensive denial or stubborn refusal to embrace the truly radical nature of the conceptualist project- the privileging of the question of how things mean."[147] I argue that even though conceptualists may have failed in their attempt to avoid commodification, they succeeded in demonstrating the extent of commodification in our culture, as today, conceptual works are now sold, framed, and canonized.

---

[144] Buchloh, Benjamin, "Conceptual Art 1962-1969: From the Aesthetic of Administration to the Critique of Institutions," October, no. 55, Winter 1990, 143.

[145] Pincus-Witten, Robert, Postminimalism into Maximalism: American Art, 1966-1986, Ann Arbor, 1987, 6.

[146] Buchloh, Benjamin, "Conceptual Art 1962-1969: From the Aesthetic of Administration to the Critique of Institutions," October, no. 55, Winter 1990, 143.

[147] Hixson, Kathryn, "Truth or Dare," New Art Examiner, XXIII, Sum. 1996, 23.

Earlier, I mentioned Lippard's positive and negative points concerning conceptual artists' attempts at demateri-alization. Lippard also acknowledges that conceptual art made several aesthetic contributions. "An informational, documentary idiom has provided a vehicle for art ideas that were encumbered and obscured by formal considera-tions."[148] However, Lippard has expressed personal disap-pointment overall with conceptualism. Conceptual art seemed to hold potential politically and socially as it did not require expensive materials and so was open as a medi-um to everyone. But she now describes "the trip from oil on canvas to ideas" as:

> another instance of 'downward mobility' or middle class guilt. It was no accident that Conceptual Art appeared at the height of the social movements of the late 1960's nor that the artists were sympath-etic to those movements.[149]

Conceptualism was rebellious in its questioning of the gallery system and examination of the nature of art, how-ever, only the rich could afford to waste money on art that might not last and was not decorative; "non-object art was only good if you already had too many possessions."[150] In his *Conceptual Art*, Godfrey says that artists had been naïve in thinking that art did not always start off as a com-modity, and as art and the market were married, one could not hold an anti-art position.[151] Lippard was disappointed at conceptualism's being swallowed by the art market, and she has since looked back to describe the whole phe-nomenon as elitist despite the revolutionary intent of those involved. What they did not understand was it alienated the people "out there" with its complexity, "no matter how fashionably downwardly mobile it might be in the art

[148] Lippard, Lucy R., *Six Years: The Dematerialization of the Art Object from 1966 to 1972*, New York, 1973, 263.

[149] Lippard, Lucy, *The Pink Glass Swan*, New York, 1995, 121.

[150] Ibid.

[151] Godfrey, Tony, *Conceptual Art*, London, 1998, 256.

world."[152] Lippard was also disappointed in its failure to break down the "real barriers between art context and those external disciplines ... from which it draws substance."[153] Many artists looked to other fields for inspiration, but there were no large collaborative efforts, no real interchanges.

By the mid-seventies, it was felt that the dematerialization had been taken too literally and too seriously. Early conceptual art in gallery spaces seemed a strange and meaningless exercise in freedom instead of responsible investigations of the conditions of making meaning. A change to a more straightforward, more political content was desired. In the 1980's, feminist artists combined the political and analytical. They demanded recognition that the audience was not homogenous, but instead diverse in gender, race, and background. These differences meant different meanings. Artists like Mary Kelly saw previous conceptual art as having several major flaws, such as generalizing the audience, using an authoritative voice, and failing to give the artist's social and economical place. But these feminist artists still utilize techniques developed by the conceptualists. So while the conceptualists did not take into account social concerns and issues of perspective diversity, they did set the foundation for work that did and developed methodologies that would aid that work.

In the 1960's, conceptual artists had tried to present new relationships with information. This trend lost momentum in the 1970's though it was kept alive by a few artists. In the 1980's, artists revived the use of the concept as a work of art, but paired this with a cynicism of the materiality in culture. While it had seemed natural to the conceptual artists of the sixties to remove the object from their work, the neo-conceptualists embraced the object with all its evils. It had seemed obvious to artists in the sixties that after minimalism's simplicity of the object, the next step should be to get rid of the object. The neo-conceptualists placed great importance on the idea, but they utilized different forms of expression to do so. Since the

---

[152] Lippard, Lucy, *The Pink Glass Swan*, New York, 1995, 121.

[153] Lippard, Lucy R., *Six Years: The Dematerialization of the Art Object from 1966 to 1972*, New York, 1973, 263.

mid-1980's, there has been a huge influx of neo-conceptual and post-conceptual art into the art market. Most of this has been a recycling of earlier conceptual art and its themes. Much of it has the same clean look as conceptual art, but unlike conceptual art it is mainly concerned with luxury goods.

Robert Morgan makes a distinction concerning the art of the new generation of conceptualists. In addition to the still working conceptualists, he adds two classifications: neo-conceptualists and post-conceptualists. Post-conceptualists refers to the generation of artists after the conceptualists who began to utilize the traditional techniques of conceptual art to set up a critical relationship with objects.[154] Neo-conceptualism could also be defined commodity conceptualism; it indulges in the commodity from a critical standpoint, using corporate glut as raw material.[155] It emerged to popularity in the 1980's, allied with popular culture and conceptual art, as a reflection on the status of the object.[156] A prime example of a neo-conceptualist is Jeff Koons, whose techniques can be seen as radically different from Louis Lawler, who is herself defined by Morgan as a post-conceptualist. The latter is concerned with historical advance where as the former is not, he striving for publicity, sales, and "the categories necessary to legitimize [his] entrance into the code of signs."[157] The work of these two artists will be examined in the next section.

Tony Godfrey believes that conceptual art has recently stopped its questioning of art and the institutions surrounding it, and has instead focused on the artists as autobiography.[158] Though he believes conceptual art continues, he cites *Documenta V* exhibition of 1972 in Kassel as the

---

[154] Morgan, Robert C., Conceptual Art: An American Perspective, London, 1994, 125.

[155] Ibid., 126.

[156] Newman, Michael, "An Unfinshed Project?" *Kunst and Museumjournaal,* VII, 1996, 9.

[157] Morgan, Robert C., Conceptual Art: An American Perspective, London, 1994128.

[158] Bird, Jon and Michael Newman, *Rewriting Conceptual Art*, London, 1999, 9.

end of conceptualism as a distinct phenomenon. This large exhibition was organized into categories in order to make it more manageable, however many of the artists resented the categories, feeling they were forced to conform to the idea of the curator. Harald Szeemann, one of the curators, declared in the catalog that the work of the artists were of another world.[159] This implied that art had ceased to be an important element in contemporary society. Godfrey noted "Art's revolutionary or subversive character was minimized and absorbed, to the extent it now seemed little more than a tool in the arsenal of the establishment."[160] Conceptual art had become the new academy, the thing it had originally fought against. The moment is similar to Duchamp having to withdraw his *Nude Descending a Staircase (No. 2)* from the Salon des Independents, the artist realizing the avant-garde could be as tyrannical, once accepted, as the academy. Godfrey makes the distinction that if conceptual art is a coherent movement whose purpose was to destroy the gallery system, than it has fizzled out. However, if it is seen as something less clearly delineated, than we can view it as "being sustained, perhaps less visibly, in various places and various ways."[161] Through the continuing efforts of artists like Kosuth and Weiner, works are still being made which meet the original criteria of conceptual art, demonstrating its vitality.

Godfrey finds differences in the conceptual art of the 1960's and that of today, seeing the work of today being done in a cleaner manner, though not with the same poignancy and complexity. He also argues that conceptual art of the 1960's was a failure as it did not meet its utopian goals, and the new generation differs in its setting realistic goals. He cites Barbara Kruger, who said, "I don't think about conceptual art ... I prefer effectivity to sadly deluded romanticism."[162] He qualifies this by quoting Victor

---

[159] Kurtz, bruce, "Documenta 5: A Critical Preview," *Arts Magazine*, XLVI, Sum. 1972, 30.

[160] Godfrey, Tony, *Conceptual Art*, London, 1998, 251.

[161] Ibid., 258.

[162] Ibid., 382.

Burgin, a British conceptualist who worked in the late sixties and early seventies.

> The original conceptual art ... is a failed avant-garde. Historians will not be surprised to find, amongst the ruins of its Utopian program, the desire to resist commodification and assimilation to a history of styles. The "new" conceptualism is the mirror image of the old-*nothing but commodity, nothing but style.* We once again have occasion to observe, "What history plays the first time around as tragedy, it repeats as farce."[163]

In these words, there is a bitter tone, perhaps stemming from the admittance of failure, but also perhaps from a younger generation threatening to overshadow the older.

Like Godfrey, Thomas Crow believes conceptual art has failed to meet its goals. Postmodern theory has strengthened the art world's attachments to painting and sculpture, as the art market is more accustomed to selling these objects.[164] This has caused a resurgence in the popularity of visual works as opposed to idea-based works. Crow also believes that the conceptualists' aspirations have been further diminished by a loss of support from critics, many of whom agree that the period is over. Benjamin Buchloh described conceptual art as having an enlightened triumph that has been short lived in its abolition of the object and has given way to the return of painterly and sculptural paradigms of the past.[165] Charles Harrison, a member of the Art and Language group, believed conceptual art must foster a changed sense of the greater public alongside its transformation of practice. But he found that even his own group reached limited success on these criteria as it could identify no alternative public other than its

---

[163] Ibid., 386.

[164] Crow, Thomas, *Modern Art in the Common Culture*, New Haven, 1996, 215.

[165] Ibid.

own participants. Crow acknowledges these opinions, saying:

> If the history of conceptual art is to maintain a critical value in relation to the apparent triumph of visuality, it must meet the conditions implied in their [Buchloh and Harrison's] judgement on its fate: 1) it must be living and available rather than concluded; 2) it must presuppose, at least in its imaginative reach, renewed contact with lay audiences; and 3) it must document a capacity for significant reference to the work beyond the most proximate institutions of artistic display and consumption.[166]

Crow believes that there are contemporary artists who meet these criteria, citing Christopher Williams and Bas Jan Ader. I would exclude Ader from this list, he having disappeared sailing in 1975 and therefore not creating works past the decline of conceptual art. The works of Williams will be discussed later in this section. To this list I would like to add some names familiar to this essay: Kosuth, Weiner, and LeWitt. These three artists have continued their original tactics but have continued to reach a greater audience. And in addition to these established conceptualists, I believe conceptual art has been created by the neo-conceptualists and post-conceptualists.

---

[166] Ibid., 216.

The Next Generation

Crow champions the work of Christopher Williams as an example of an artist whose conceptual work continues to maintain a critical value. Williams' work as it evolved through the 1980's held the archive as its main subject. His typical process is to create a set of clearly defined rules of selection from a body of images. One of his well-known pieces is made of photographs taken from the photographic archive at the John F. Kennedy Library. The photographs he has selected must meet two conditions: they must be dated May 10, 1963, and the subject must be John F. Kennedy with his back to the camera. Williams rephotographs these images, enlarges them, and crops the picture. The tittle of the work includes information of the source of the photographs, the conditions for selection, the technical treatment of the images, and how the photographs are presented, which varies as it includes the name and date of the exhibition, and the name and address of the venue. The work reveals a strict process of documentation reminiscent of early conceptual works, but also recognizes, as Crow says, "meaning on the level of historical folk memory."[167] The work does so by using images taken in the year of Kennedy's death, reminding the viewer of this tragedy while at the same time appearing cold in its material and presentation. There is a lack of excess, illusion, and fiction making the work poignant in its straightforward relationship with the reader. Williams' work demonstrates that conceptual art has not concluded, using the documentary techniques of the early conceptualists to describe popular subjects that renew contact with lay audiences and making reference outside of the institutions of artistic display and consumption. Jeff Wall does something similar through his use of staged photographs.

Jeff Wall is an artist who, though he lives in Vancouver, I feel is worth citing due to his proximity to the United States and his notoriety. Working in the early sev-

---

[167] Crow, Thomas, *Modern Art in the Common Culture*, New Haven, 1996, 198.

enties with photography and text, he spent the next few years in postgraduate study in art history in London. References to his studies can be seen in the back-lit photographic transparencies which made a name for him in the late seventies as his signature format. He has declared that "none of my work could have been done without the turmoil in art history," which evoke references to painting in their mural size. [168] Also the intricate staging of his photographic subjects is similar to the painter's attention to composition and technical refinement without having to resort to quotations. An example is *The Guitarist*, which portrays the disorder of a teenager's room filled with graffiti that encompasses hippie, punk, and hardcore youth cultures which predate the occupants and demonstrate vernacular collage while its context suggests a dada tradition. Crow notes that Wall uses a dark haired Guatemalan girl "to join Manet's Latin guitarists and dancers, the painter's response to the fascination exerted by the touring Spanish troupes of the 1860's."[169] Crow goes on to explain that the connection is pertinent as Manet "himself having used these entertainers to collapse the historical distance between his own moment and the tradition of Spanish tonal painting of Velazquez to Goya."[170] Recently, Wall has taken to partially synthesizing his photographs, using computers to create scenes which he says could not be made otherwise. The vividness of his images with their dense historical background has put him on the lists of many critics, like Burhhard Riemschneider and Uta Grosenick, as one of the most innovative living artists, and as one of the top ten living artists by *Artnews* magazine, along with Bruce Nauman (December, 1999). Though his work is constantly evolving, Wall still sees himself as coming from and continuing the tradition of conceptualism.

---

[168] Clark, Guilbaut, and Wagner, "Representations Suspicions, and Critical Transparency: an interview with Jeff Wall," *Parachute,* LIX, July-Sept. 1990, 10.

[169] Crow, Thomas, *Modern Art in the Common Culture*, New Haven, 1996, 164.

[170] Ibid.

Many new artists in the eighties used, diverted, and segmented accepted facts of conceptual art.[171] Artists such as Res Ingold outside of America use similar methods to the conceptualists, making artworks into a kind of game where the object is a kind of punchline. Advertising information for his *Ingold Airlines* appear to be a readymade object, a brochure stand, yet it holds a signature and is part of a series. Inspired by Yves Klein, Ingold's paraphernalia has appeared in galleries, museums, and fairs, presenting the image of a full grown airline company. However, it was in August of 1990 when the eight-year-old company made its first flight between two Dutch towns, making the project that had been about possibility into an actual operation with a combination of humor and seriousness, freedom and industry, creativity and function operating within the art world. The artist has mimicked production, embracing the object, not simply finding it. While conceptual art tried to transcend modernism, this new conceptual art seems to hold a super naivete, as if to say "I made this to look like everything else I see."

Jeff Koons is another artist who borrows from the tradition of conceptual art and the readymade. In the 1980's, he was seen as a power hungry, corporate culture icon. He runs his studio like a business, with anywhere from 35-70 assistants who fill in his paintings as if they were painting-by-numbers.[172] He produces images of objects with which people have grown up and can identify, objects that have had an impact on people's lives though they appear frivolous. His works, like Ingold's, sometimes hold the appearance of a readymade, such as a ceramic *Pink Panther* or *Michael Jackson with Bubbles*, but they are careful reproductions, fusing kitsch objects with a labor that gives paintings their fetish quality. They also remark on commodity culture and the prevalence of materialism in our lives. Koons acknowledges his work as linked to conceptualism, but he believes he does more than the conceptualists have done. He views earlier conceptual art as too cerebral,

---

[171] Bourriaud, Nicolas, "The Signature Game," *Flash Art*, no.155, Nov./Dec. 1990, 126.

[172] Attias, Laurie, "A Kinder Gentler Koons," *Artnews*, XCVII, Mar. 1998, 158.

where his work settles cerebral needs, but also needs of se-
curity and sexuality.[173] Unlike the conceptualists, he does
not study theory, but instead studies the culture around
him.[174] He compares his work to advertising: it keeps you
interested and stays in your head with the mechanics hidden behind it.[175] It does not alienate the viewer in its intel-
lectualism as conceptualism did. This is an important distinction between Koons' work and the conceptualists in
that Koons tries to hide his ideas behind the object, and
the conceptualists threw out the object to present their
message more directly. So critics, like Gregorio Magnani,
say that Koons' work demands to be read as conceptual,
but it is hard to identify the content as meaning is only
given in relationships.[176]

In his *Passeagen-Werk*, Benjamin argued how objects
from consumer culture just slightly out of date held a re-
sidual critical power, deifying the enforced amnesia necessary for the marketplace to operate smoothly. Koons'
works, as well as the works of Louise Lawler, often hold
this critical position. Since the late 1970's, Lawler has photographed works of art as they are displayed in exhibitions
or in private settings, in particular modernist works and
works by her own generation. Through her photographs,
Lawler shows the "desacrilization" of the art object and the
aura of the degraded work caused by serial reproduction.[177]
Her work is an example of appropriation art, an offshoot
of conceptualism's documentary aspects. She is interested
not in the pictorial content, aesthetic expression, or historical value of the works she documents, but in investigating
the objectivity of the work as a thing in context, studying
the work after it leaves the studio, with each new frame of
presentation meaning different functional relations, the

[173] Koons, Jeff, "Conceptual Art of the 60's and 70's Alienated
the Viewer," *Flash Art*, no. 143, Nov./Dec. 1988, 113.

[174] Ibid.

[175] Ibid.

[176] Magnani, Gregorio, "This is Not Conceptual," *Flash Art*, no.
145, Mar./Apr. 1989, 85.

[177] Ball, Edward, "The Beautiful Language of my Century," *Arts
Magazine*, LXIII, Jan. 1989, 65.

work often being co-opted by interests alien to art.[178] Her work shows art as part of an economic system, but also presents aesthetic values, often using Warhol as an example of art submitting to a capitalist market.[179] She constructs a counter-position to curators from which she can comment on the art world and its aesthetic, institutional, and commercial structures. Similar to the earlier conceptualists, she uses her camera as a recording instrument to gather evidence and also similarly her work expresses dissatisfaction in the role of artist as solo adventurer, preferring to construct a reactionary ideology of the artist as one who reveals the truth.[180]

Like Lawler, the artist Mary Kelly is a prime example of the change in conceptualist thought in the eighties. She utilizes conceptual art strategies in order to look at issues dealing with representation, and specifically with the construction of the representation of women.[181] It has been pointed out that in America, the realm of conceptual art has belonged to a white patriarchy, and Kelly has questioned the authority of the language they use in her work. [182] Her *Post Partum Document* of 1973-1979 is a reaction against conceptual art exhibitions by Weiner, Graham, and Art and Language.[183] She appropriated the clean, impersonal format of conceptual art and used it to display infant souvenirs often fetishized, documented by a diary of a mother weaning off her baby. This kind of feminist reevaluation of subjectivity has served as a catalyst for going beyond questions of gender, class and sex that post-conceptualists criticize conceptualists for not addressing. Artists such as Kelly, Lothar Baumgarten, Alfredo Jaar,

---

[178] Elger and Weski, "Behind the Art Scene with Louise Lawler," *Louise Lawler for Sale,* Ostfilden, Germany, 1994.

[179] Ibid.

[180] Cameron, Dan, "Art and its Double," *Flash Art,* no.134, May 1987, 72.

[181] Ibid., 96.

[182] Ibid., 97.

[183] Kelly, Mary, "To Deconstruct the Notion of Masculine and Feminine," *Flash Art,* no. 143, Nov./Dec. 1988, 114.

Silvia Kolbowski, and Barbara Krueger use conceptual art strategies and the art world as an arena to examine these issues.

The neo-conceptualists and post-conceptualists were not the only contemporary artists that have been influenced by conceptualism. An example is Tom Friedman, who works in western Massachusetts. Friedman has shown in the Saatchi Gallery in London and the Institute of Contemporary Art in Boston. Most of his works are untitled, but they are typically described by their materials. And it is conceptualism that opened the field of what could be used to make art. Friedman has made sculptures out of masking tape, pencils, a bucket of straws, bubble gum, and other seemingly normal material. But he plays with the context of what the art object appears to be and what it is. Looking at one of his untitled sculptures, it would appear that the pedestal holds nothing, but the wall-copy reveals that sculpture consists of a cubic foot of air cursed by a witch. Another sculpture might appear to be a 2x4 piece of wood, but a glance at the materials listed on the plaque beside it reveals it is a 2x4 painted meticulously to look like a 2x4. The list of media becomes the documentation of the idea that would otherwise go unnoticed. Seemingly plain objects are actually the conclusions of meaningful and arduous processes while his examination of materials is comparable to Bruce Nauman or Robert Morris. His work, while not appearing to look like conceptual art, has a flavor of many of the basic tenets of conceptual art. One is the importance of the idea in his work. He has embraced the object in order to demonstrate the difference between what we see and what we think we see.

Another example of an artist indebted to conceptual artists, but at the same time not working in their footsteps is Jenny Holzer. Her most famous works consist of text running across LCD signs and has been shown in the Guggenheim in Bilboa and New York, in the Museum of Fine Arts of Boston, and numerous other museums. Her signs consist of short phrases in different languages running across them. She has been criticized for the shallowness of her messages and for imitating conceptualism without advancing it. She says she does not consider herself a conceptualist and believes herself to have come before the neo-conceptualist. She appreciates early conceptualism as it made the mind in art respectable, but says she has not studied conceptual art in great depth.[184] She does not study theory or history, but she sees how much of her work has been informed by conceptualism.[185] In a 1994 exhibition in the Barbara Gladstone gallery in New York, she installed a cave like structure made from red leather and with LCD signs emitting phrases concerning rape. Critic Laura Cottingham complained that its lack of complexity and dimension caused the installation to fail as both art and politic.[186] The lack of a dimension of complex theory separates Holzer from the conceptualists, though she uses text as a visual medium. She appears to be an example of one who assumed the appearance of conceptual art without examining the idea structure behind it.

What is important is not the amount of accolade critics give artists such as Ingold, Williams, Kelly, Friedman, or Koons but simply that these new artists working in the tradition of the conceptualists, and others like them, are a force in the art world. When Koons installed his topiary of a puppy in front of the new Guggenhiem in Bilboa, it was an event people could not stop talking about. The neo- and post-conceptualists are surrounded by controversy and their works are widely discussed, and these works are based on themes taken directly from conceptual art. It is conceptual art's influence that has caused artists and critics to continually push the boundaries of what is art, to question the value of the object, and the importance of the idea verses the visual. These are issues first addressed directly by Duchamp, and have been continuously addressed through the apex of conceptualism and beyond. It has reshaped how we view art, looking not simply for physical beauty or emotional content in works, but also for intellectual stimulation. It is the reason people ask as they view a picture, "Why is this art?" and "What does this mean?"

---

[184] Holzer, Jenny, "Language Communicates," *Flash Art*, no. 143, Nov./Dec. 1988, 112.

[185] Ibid.

[186] Cottingham, Laura, "Jenny Holzer," *Flash Art*, XXVII, Oct. 1994, 91.

6. Conclusion

Kempton Mooney

Conceptual art was a gradually developing medium that took its first major steps in the works of Marcel Duchamp. Over the course of the twentieth century, a number of artists created works that were largely conceptual, but it was the mid-1960's when these works were first called conceptual. Not until then were artists creating such works in a volume that would justify a category being devoted to the medium. The phenomenon of multiple artists creating idea-based works resulted in the beginning of conceptualism, despite conceptual art's already having been developed by artists like Henry Flynt and Ed Kienholz. This paper has been by no means a description of all the conceptualists who were involved in American conceptualism, but rather a demonstration of the variety of paths taken by the major contributors to American conceptualism. Some examined the art world, questioning the fetish value of high culture. Some looked outside the art world to other academic sources of knowledge, such as science or philosophy, or to mass culture to celebrate works from these roots as a part of art. And some rejected the commodity and art traditions completely in an effort free creativity from the restrictions of the commercial institution of art. The reader may note that all of those mentioned as American conceptualists were white men. This is representative of the majority of the conceptualists, despite conceptualism's potential to be created by anyone due to the little physical materials it required.

While challenging the museum and gallery establishment as well as traditional ideas of art, conceptual art became widely popular. Many of its artists became superstars. The notoriety of these artists led to conceptual art becoming a major trend, an institution similar to those it had first tried to challenge. This has led many of its followers and critics to ask how successful have the makers of conceptual art been in attaining their goals.

Throughout this paper, I have cited the beliefs of many critics on conceptual art. I myself believe conceptual art has and will continue to be used successfully by many artists. I also believe that these artists have attained many of the goals that led them to use conceptual art. They brought attention to how art is constructed, shown and received. They also helped obtain freedom for artists to use any process they deemed necessary. And though conceptualism did decline, it examined art and subsequent generations can learn from these examinations. In this way, conceptual art will always affect us, as maintained by the large number of today's artists influenced by the conceptualists' work.[187] Though there has been a decline in the emphasis of intellectual art over visual art and the questioning of the museum and gallery institution, conceptualism brought awareness to the art scene of the United States and set a foundation for artists to continue to educate themselves and their audience about the nature of art.

---

[187] In *Art at the Turn of the Millennium,* Riemschneider and Grosenick list 137 artists to suggest the directions in which the art of the near future is heading. Twenty three of these artists are described as influenced by the conceptualists in some way, including Jeff Koons, Jenny Holzer, Jeff Wall, Barbara Krueger, Cindy Sherman, Art Club 2000, and General Idea. *Art at the Turn of the Millennium,* ed. Burkhard Riemschneider and Uta Grosenick, New York, 1999.

Works Consulted

General Sources

"A. Reinhardt, J. Kosuth, F. Gonzalez Torres: Symptoms of Interference, Conditions of Possibility," *Art and Design*, IX, Jan./ Feb. 1994, p. 6-96. Special issue containing seventeen articles on the three artists.

Art History and Its Methods, ed. Eric Fernie, London, 1998.

Art of the Twentieth Century, ed. Ingo F. Walther, Koln, 1998.

Art Since Mid-Century: The New Internationalism, with contributions by Werner Haftmann (and others), Greenwich, 1971.

Atkins, Robert, *Artspeak,* New York, 1997.

Archer, Michael, *Art Since 1960,* London, 1997.

Crow, Thomas, *Modern Art in the Common Culture,* New Haven, 1996.

Fineberg, Jonathan, *Art Since 1940: Strategies of Being,* Upper Saddle River,1995.

Harrison, Charles and Paul Wood, *Art in Theory: 1900-1990,* Oxford, 1998. Excellent collection of primary sources.

Hauser, Arnold, *The Social History of Art: Naturalism, Impressionism, The Film Age,* London, 1999.

Heywood, Ian, *Social Theories of Art: A Critique,* New York, 1997.

Hunter, Sam and John Jacobus, *Modern Art,* New York, 1992.

Janson, H. W., *History of Art,* New York, 1995

Lippard, Lucy, *The Pink Glass Swan,* New York, 1995.

Modern Art and Popular Culture: Readings in High and Low, ed. Kirk Varnedoe and Adam Gopnik, New York, 1990.

The New Art, ed. Gregory Battcock, New York, 1966.

Pincus-Witten, Robert, *Postminimalism,* New York, 1977.

Pincus-Witten, Robert, *Postminimalism into Maximalism: American Art, 1966-1986,* Ann Arbor, 1987.

Stokstad, Marilyn, *Art History,* New York, 1999.

Precursors

Dada

Ball, Hugo, "Dada Fragments" (1916-1917), *Flucht aus der Zeit (Flight from Time)*, Munich and Leipzig, 1927, English translation in Motherwell, Robert R., ed., *The Dada Painters and Poets*, New York, *1951*.

Benjamin, Walter, "The Author as Producer" (1934), English translation in Bostock, Anna, ed., *Understanding Brecht*, London, 1983. Benjamin first delivered "The Author as Producer" as a lecture on April 27, 1934 to the Institute for the Study of Fascism. The present version is taken from the first English translation by Anna Bostock.

Huelsenbeck, Richard, *En Avant Dada* (1920), English translation in Motherwell, Robert R., ed., *The Dada Painters and Poets*, New York, *1951*.

Tzara, Tristan, "Dada Manifesto 1918" (1918), English translation in Motherwell, Robert R., ed., *The Dada Painters and Poets*, New York, *1951*.

Frankfurt School

Adorno, Theodor, *Minima Moralia*, New York, 1999.

Benjamin, Walter, *Illuminations*, New York, 1969. Includes the essay "The Work of Art in the Age of Mechanical Reproduction" (1936).

Horkheimer, Max and Theodor Adorno, *Dialectic of Enlightenment*, New York, 1997.

Huyssen, Andreas, *After the Great Divide*, Indianapolis, 1986.

Reinhardt

Reinhardt, Ad, "Art as Art" (1962), in *Art as Art: the Selected Writings of Ad Reinhardt*, ed. B. Rose, New York, 1972.

Corris, Michael, "Ad Reinhardt: The Invisible College of Conceptual Art" *Flash Art*, XXVII, Oct.,1994, p. 49-52.

Fluxus

An Anthology, ed. Young and MacLaw, New York, 1962.

Hendricks, Jon, *Fluxus Codex,* cat., The Gilbert and Lila Silverman Fluxus Collection, Detroit, 1988.

Higgins, Dick, *Modernism Since Postmodernism: Essays on Intermedia*, San Diego, 1997.

Phillpot, Clive, *Fluxus*, exh. cat., Museum of Modern Art, New York, 1988.

Smith, Owen, *Fluxus: The History of Attitude*, San Diego, 1998.

Minimalism

Batchelor, David, *Minimalism,* Cambridge, 1997.

Biggs, Lewis, Penelope Curtis, and Jemima Pyne, *Minimalism*, exh. cat., Tate Gallery Liverpool, Liverpool,1989.

Carmean, E. A., *The Great Decade of American Abstraction*, exh. cat., Museum of Fine Arts, Houston, 1974.

Conceptual Art in America

General

"Artists Protest Sponsorship," *Artnews*, VC, Feb. 1996, p. 53.

"The Duchamp Effect," *October*, no. 70, Fall 1994, p. 3-146. Thirteen article special edition which includes the article "Conceptual Art and the Reception of Duchamp."

"Homer Simpson," *Flash Art*, XXXII, Sum. 1999, p. 75.

"Line as Langauge," *Artnews*, LXXIII, Sum. 1974, p. 113-114. Review of exhibit organized by Rosalind Krauss containing works by Bochner, LeWitt, Morris, and Rockburne.

"Picasso: A Symposium," *Art in America*, LXVIII, Dec. 1980, p. 9-187. Contains contributions from John Jacobus, Joseph Kosuth, and others who address conceptual art directly.

Artwords 2: Discourse on the Early 80's, ed. Jeanne Siegel, Ann Arbor, 1988. Interviews with Laurie Anderson, John Baldessari, Hans Haacke, Joseph Beuys, Sherry Levine, Jenny Holzer, and Barbara Krueger.

Battcock, Gregory, *Idea Art*, New York, 1973.

Bird, Jon and Michael Newman, *Rewriting Conceptual Art*, London, 1999.

Buchloh, Benjamin, "Conceptual Art 1962-1969: From the Aesthetic of Administration to the Critique of Institutions," *October*, no. 55, Winter 1990, p. 103-143.

Buchloh, Benjamin, "Reply to Joseph Kosuth and Seth Siegelaub," *October*, no. 57, Sum. 1991, p. 152-161.

Burn, Ian, "The 1960's: Crisis and Aftermath," *Writings in Art History*, North Sydney, 1991.

Do It, cat., Independent Curators Inc., New York, 1997. Catalog of word-based pieces without a gallery exhibition.

Frackman, Noel, "Documenta 7," *Arts Magazine*, LVII, October, 1982, p. 91-97.

Flash Art, XXI, Nov./Dec. 1988, p. 87-117. Contains a supplement on conceptual art.

Godfrey, Tony, *Conceptual Art*, London, 1998.

Global Conceptualism: Points of Origin, 1950's-1980's, exh. cat., ed. Philomena Mariani, Queens Museum of Art, New York, 1999.

Harrison, Charles, *Essays on Art and Language*, Cambridge, 1991.

Hixson, Kathryn, "Truth or Dare," *New Art Examiner*, XXIII, Sum. 1996, p. 18-23.

January 5-31, 1969, exh. cat., Seth Siegelaub, New York, 1969.

Karlen, Peter H., "Protecting Conceptual Art," *Artweek*, IIXX, Dec. 12 1987, p. 14.

Kyauss, Rosalind and Yve-Alain Bois, "A User's Guide To Entropy," *October*, no. 78, Fall 1996, p. 38-88.

Kozloff, Max, "Pygmalian Reversed," *Artforum*, XIV, Nov. 1975, p. 30-37. Discusses Graham, Oppenheim, and Baldessari.

Lieberman, Rhonda, "Barbara Krueger," *Flash Art*, XXIV, May/June 1991, p. 139.

Lippard, Lucy R., *Six Years: The Dematerialization of the Art Object from 1966 to 1972*, New York, 1973. Documents exhibitions, publications, interviews, and works by conceptualists.

Meyer, Ursula, *Conceptual Art*, New York, 1972.

Morgan, Robert C., *Conceptual Art: An American Perspective*, London, 1994.

Morgan, Robert C., "The Situation of Conceptual," *Arts Magazine,* LXIII, Feb. 1989, p. 40-50.

Morgan, Robert C., *Art into Ideas: Essays on Conceptual Art.* Cambridge [England], 1996.

Morgan, Robert C., "The Role of Documentation in Conceptual Art," Ph.D. diss., New

York University, New York, 1978.

Nittve, L., "Ars '83," *Artforum,* XXII, April 1984, p. 92.

O'Doherty, Brian, "The Gallery as a Gesture," *Artforum,* XIX, Dec. 1981, p. 26-34. Describes work by Robert Barry.

Oldenberg, Claus, "America: War and Sex, Etc.," *Arts Magazine,* XLI, Sum., 1967, p. 32-38.

On Kawara: Date Painting in 89 Cities, exh. cat., Museum Boymans-van Beuningen, Amsterdam, 1992.

Perrault, John, "Art Disturbances," *The Village Voice,* Jan. 25, 1969, 14-18.

Perrone, Jeff, "Words: When Art Takes a Rest," *Artforum,* XV, Sum. 1977, p. 36-37. Describes *Words* show at Whitney, critiques Baldessari.

Pincus-Witten, Robert, "Theater of the Conceptual," *Artforum,* XI, Oct. 1973, p. 40-46.

Piper, Adrian, "Ian Burn's Conceptualism," *Art in America,* LXXXV, Dec. 1997, p. 72-79.

Plagens, Peter, "Review of *557,087,*" *Artforum,* VII, Nov. 1969, p. 64-67.

Raffaele, Joseph and E. C. Baker, "Way-Out West," *Artnews,* LXVI, Sum. 1967, p. 38-40.

Renten, Andrew, "Robert Barry," *Flash Art,* XXIV, May/June 1991, p. 122-125.

Robert Lehman Lectures on Contemporary Art, ed. Lynne Cooke and Karen Kelly, New York, 1996.

Stimson, Paul, "Between the Signs," *Art in America,* LXIII, Oct. 1979, p. 80-81.

Smithson, Robert, "Quasi-Infinities and the Waning of Space," *Arts Magazine,* XLI, Nov. 1966, p. 28-31.

Shirey, David, "Thinkworks," *Art in America,* LVII, May/June 1969, p. 39-40. Describes works by Huebler, Barry, Kienholz, and Kosuth.

Tomkins, Calvin, "The Art World: An End to Chauvanism," *New Yorker,* LVII, Dec. 7, 1981, p. 146. Describes works by Huebler.

van den Bergh, Jos, "Roman Opalka: Opaque Addition," *Flash Art,* XXIV, May/June 1991, p. 132.

Vetrocq, Martha E., "Conceptualism: An Expanded View," *Art in America,* LXXXVII, July 1999, p. 72-77.

John Baldessari

Clifford, Katie, "John Baldessari," *Artnews,* XCVII, Apr. 1998, p. 176.

Collins, James, "Pointing, Hybrids, And Romanticism: John Baldessari," *Artforum,* XI, Oct. 1973, p. 53-58.

Drohojowski, Hunter, "No More Boring Art," *Artnews,* LXXXV, Jan. 1986, p. 62-69.

Lichtenstein, Therese, Review, *Flash Art,* XIX, Sum. 1986, p. 68.

Rubinfien, Leo, "Through Western Eyes," *Art in America,* LXVI, Sept./Oct. 1978, p. 75-77.

Salvioni, Daniela, "Letters from France," *Arts Magazine,* LXIII, Sum. 1989, p. 105-106.

van Bruggen, Coosje, *John Baldessari,* New York, 1990.

Winer, Helene, "Scenarios/ Documents/ Images I," *Art in America,* LXI, Mar. 1973, p. 42-47.

Mel Bochner

Boice, Bruce, "Axiom of Indifference," *Arts Magazine*, XLVII, Apr. 1973, p. 66-68.

Lichtenstein, Therese, "Mel Bochner," *Arts Masgazine*, LVIII, Dec. 1983, p. 34-35.

Bochner, Mel, "Alfaville," *Arts Magazine*, v. XLII, May 1968, p. 14-17.

Bochner, Mel, "Serial Art Systems," *Arts Magazine*, XLI, Sum. 1967, p. 39-43.

Bochner, Mel, "Beach Boys-'100%,'" *Arts Magazine*, XLI, Mar. 1967, p. 24.

Bochner, Mel, "Systemic," *Arts Magazine*, XLI, Nov. 1966, p. 40.

Field, Richard S., *Mel Bochner: Thought Made Visible 1966-1973*, exh. cat., Yale University Art Gallery, New Haven, 1995.

Jarmusch, Ann, "Freewheeling Diversity," *Artnews*, LXXVII, Sep. 1978, p. 134.

Krauss, Rosalind, "Sense and Sensibilty," *Artforum*, XII, Nov. 1973, p. 43-53.

Meyer, James, "The Gallery is a Theater," *Flash Art*, XXVII, Sum. 1994, p. 99-142.

Dan Graham

"Dan Graham at John Gibson," *Arts Magazine*, XLV, Feb. 1971, p. 58.

Buchloh, Benjamin, "Allegorical Procedures: Appropriation and Montage in Contemporary Art," *Artforum*, XXI, Sep. 1982, p. 43-56.

Graham, Dan, "Carl Andre," *Arts Magazine*, XLI, Dec./Jan. 1967, p. 34-35.

Graham, Dan, "Intention Intentionality Sequence," *Arts Magazine*, XLVII, Apr. 1973, p. 64.

Graham, Dan, "Models and Monuments," *Arts Magazine,* XLI, Mar. 1967, p. 32-35.

Graham, Dan, *Rock My Religion: Writings and Projects 1965-90*, Cambridge, MA, 1993.

Graham, Dan, "Two Consciousness Projection(s)," *Arts Magazine*, XLIX, Dec. 1974, p. 63.

Matthias, Rosemary, "Galleries: Dan Graham," *Arts Magazine*, LVVII, Sept./Oct. 1972, p. 59.

Doug Huebler

"Douglas Huebler," *New Art Examiner*, XXV, Sept. 1997, p. 19.

Douglas Huebler: 'Variables' Etc, exh. cat., FRAC, 1992.

Huebler, Doug and Budd Hopkins, "Concept vs. Object Art," *Arts Magazine,* XLVI, Apr. 1972, p. 50. A conversation.

Huebler, Doug, "Saboteur or Trophy? Advance or Retreat?" *Artforum*, XX, May 1982, p. 72-76.

Kosuth, Joseph, "Times of Our Lives: Remembering Douglas Huebler," *Artforum*, XXXVI, Nov. 1997, p. 15-16.

Stimson, Paul, "Fictive Escapades," *Art in America*, LV, Feb. 1982, p. 96-99.

Joseph Kosuth

"Kosuth in Europa," *Domus*, no. 585, Aug 1979, p. 53.

"Kunsthalle Bielefeld," *Domus*, no. 626, Mar. 1982, p. 74. Exhibition review.

Baker, Elizabeth, "Joseph Kosuth: Information Please," *Artnews,* LVVII, Feb. 1973, p. 30-31.

Boice, Bruce, "Joseph Kosuth: Two Shows," *Artforum,* XI, Mar. 1973, p. 84-85.

Bordaz, J. P., "Galerie Eric Fabre," *Flash Art,* no. 111, Mar. 1983, p. 69.

Castle, Ted, "Bouquet of Mistakes," *Flash Art,* XVI, Sum. 1982, p. 54.

Kosuth, Joseph, "Art After Philosophy I," *Studio International,* CLXXVIII, Oct. 1969, p. 134-137.

Kosuth, Joseph, "Art After Philosophy II," *Studio International,* CLXXVIII, Nov. 1969, p. 160-161.

Kosuth, Joseph, "Art After Philosophy III," *Studio International,* CLXXVIII, Dec. 1969, p. 212-213.

Kosuth, Joseph, *Art After Philosophy and After,* Cambridge, MA, 1991.

Kosuth, Joseph, "Intentions," *Art Bulletin,* LXXVIII, Sept. 1996, p. 407-412.

Kosuth, Joseph, "Portraits," *Artforum,* XX, May 1982, p. 58-68.

Kosuth, Joseph, *When Attitude Becomes Form,* exh. cat., March 22-April 27 1969.

Kosuth, Joseph and Seth Siegelaub, "Replies to Benjamin Buchloh on Conceptual Art," *October,* LVII, Sum. 1991, p. 152-157.

Macadam, Barbara, "A Conceptual Artist's Self-Conception," *Artnews,* XCIV, Dec. 1995, p. 124-127.

Sol LeWitt

Beck, Ernest, "Burghers Block the Box," *Artnews,* LXXXVI, Sept. 1987, p. 57.

Berger, Laurel, "In Their Sights," *Artnews*, XVI, Mar. 1997, p. 94-100.

Johnson, Ken, "Sol LeWitt," *Art in America*, LXIV, May 1990, p. 236.

Kalina, Richard, "Sol LeWitt," *Art in America*, LXXV, Nov. 1997, p. 122.

Koplos, Jenat, "El Anatsui and Sol LeWitt at Skoto," *Art in America*, LXXXV, Jan. 1997, p. 98-99.

Lapham, Lewis, "Wall Painting," *Harper's Magazine,* CCLXXV, Oct. 1987, p. 12-13.

Legg, Alicia, ed., *Sol LeWitt*,exh. cat., The Museum of Modern Art, New York, 1978.

LeWitt, Sol, *Incomplete Open Cubes*, exh.cat., The John Weber Gallery, New York, 1974.

LeWitt, Sol, "Paragraphs on Conceptual Art," *Artforum,* V, Sum. 1967, p. 79-83.

LeWitt, Sol, "Sentences on Conceptual Art" *Art-Language,* I, May 1969, p. 10-12.

LeWitt, Sol, "Ziggurnats," *Arts Magazine,* XLI, Nov. 1966, p. 24-25.

Martin, Mary Abbe, "Sol LeWitt," *Artnews*, LXXXVII, Sum. 1988, p. 194.

Morgan, Robert C., "LeWitt, Staechle, Smith," *Arts Magazine,* LXIII, Sum. 1989, p. 84.

Neff, Eileen, "Sol LeWitt, Lawrence Oliver Gallery," *Artforum*, XXVII, Mar. 1989, p. 137-138.

Reynolds, Jock, *Sol LeWitt: Twenty-Five Years of Wall Drawings*, Addison Gallery of American Art, Andover, 1993.

Sherman, Mary, "Sol LeWitt: Twenty-Five Years of Wall Drawings," *Artnews*, XCII, Nov. 1993, p. 170.

Small, Michael, "Talk About Lines," *People's Weekly*, XXVII, May 25, 1987, p. 43-44.

Stapen, Nancy, "Sol LeWitt," *Artnews*, XCIV, Jan. 1995, p. 168.

Tucker, Paul, "Sol LeWitt," *Artnews*, XCVI, Nov. 1997, p. 228.

Robert Morris

"The Artist Speaks: Robert Morris," *Art in America*, LVIII, May 1970, p. 104-111.

Robert Morris: The Mind Body Problem, exh. cat., Solomn R. Guggenheim Foundation, New York, 1994.

Robert Morris: Work of the Eighties, ed. Mary Jane Jacob and Paul Schimmel, exh. cat., Museum of Contemporary Art, Chicago, 1986.

Bruce Nauman

"Exhibition at Castelli Gallery," *Arts Magazine*, XLII, Mar. 1968, p. 62.

Bruce Nauman: exh. cat., Walker Art Center, Minneapolis, 1994.

Kurtz, B., "Documenta 5," *Arts Magazine*, XLVI, Sum. 1972, p. 42.

Livingston, Jane and Marcia Tucker, *Bruce Nauman*, New York, 1973.

Morris, Robert, "Art of Existence," *Artforum,* IX, Jan. 1971, p. 28.

Pincus-Witten, Robert, "Bruce Nauman," *Artforum*, X, Feb. 1972, p. 30-37.

Schenker, Christoph, "Bruce Nauman: Tears of a Clown," *Flash Art,* XXIV, May/June 1991, p. 126.

Tucker, M., "PheNaumanology," *Artforum,* IX, Dec. 1970, p. 38-44.

van Bruggen, Coosje, *Bruce Nauman*, New York, 1988.

Lawrence Weiner

"Leo Castelli Gallery," *Arts Magazine*,LIV, Sept. 1979, p. 34.

Alberro, Alexander and Alice Zimmerman, *Lawrence Weiner*, London, 1998.

Schwarz, Dieter, *Lawrence Weiner-Books 1968-1989. Catalogue Raisonee*, Cologne, 1989.

Giesler, D., "Different Purposes, Different Rewards," *Artweek*, XI, Mar. 1980, p. 12.

Weiner, Lawrence, "Notes from Art," *Art Journal*, XLII, Sum. 1982, p. 122-124.

Weiner, Lawrence. *Statements*. exh. cat., Seth Siegelaub, New York, 1968.

After Conceptualism

General

Art at the Turn of the Millennium, ed. Burkhard Riem-schneider and Uta Grosenick, New York, 1999.

Attias, Laurie, "A Kinder Gentler Koons," *Artnews,* XCVII, Mar. 1998, p. 158-161.

Baldwin, Michael, "Conceptual Questionaire," *Flash Art,* no. 143, Nov./Dec. 1988, p. 105-106.

Bourriaud, Nicolas, "The Signature Game," *Flash Art,* no.155, Nov./Dec. 1990, p. 126-129.

Clegg and Guttmann, "On Conceptual Art's Tradition," *Flash Art,* no. 143, Nov./Dec1988, p. 99.

Cottingham, Laura, "Jenny Holzer," *Flash Art,* XXVII, Oct. 1994, p. 94.

Holzer, Jenny, "Language Communicates," *Flash Art,* no. 143, Nov./Dec. 1988, p. 112.

Ippolito, Jon, "Where has all the Uncertainties Gone?" *Flash Art,* XXIX, Sum. 1996, p. 83.

Koons, Jeff, "Conceptual Art of the 60's and 70's Alien-ated the Viewer," *Flash Art,* no. 143, Nov./Dec. 1988, p. 113.

Kruger, Barbara, *Remote Control,* Cambridge, MA, 1998.

Magnani, Gregorio, "This is Not Conceptual," *Flash Art,* no. 145, Mar./Apr. 1989, p. 84-87.

Morgan, Robert C., "What is Conceptual Art, Post or Neo," *Arts Magazine,* LXII, Mar. 1988, p. 80-81.

Newman, Michael, "An Unfinshed Project?" *Kunst and Museumjournaal,* VII, 1996, p. 95-104.

Ramsden, Mel, "Interview," *Flash Art,* no. 143, Nov./Dec. 1988, p. 106-107.

Rimaelli, David, "It's My Party: Jeff Koons," *Artforum*, XXXV, Sum. 1997, p. 112-117.

Rush, Michael, *New Media in Late 20ᵗʰ Century Art*, New York, 1999.

Salvioni, Daniela, "Dan Graham," *Flash Art*, no. 152, May/June 1990, p. 142-144.

Staniszewski, Mary Anne, "Conceptual Art," *Flash Art*, no. 143, Nov./Dec. 1988, p. 88-99.

Tamblyn, Christine, "Computer Art as Conceptual Art," *Art Journal*, IL, Fall 1990, p. 253-256.

Tom Friedman

Canning, Susan M., "Tom Friedman," *New Art Examiner*, XXIII, Apr. 1996, p. 44-45.

Conners, Thomas, "Tom Friedman, Linda Horn," *New Art Examiner*, XXI, May 1994, p. 40-41.

Hainley, Bruce, "Next to Nothing: The Art of Tom Friedman," *Artforum*, XXXIV, Nov. 1995, p. 74-77.

Johnson, Ken, "Friedman's Flea Circus," *Art in America*, LXXXIV, May 1996, p. 78-81.

Kahn, Wolf, "Connecting Incongruities," *Art in America*, LXXX, Nov. 1992, p. 116-121.

Wilk, Deborah, "Chuck Close, Tom Friedman," *New Art Examiner*, XXIV, Sep. 1996, p. 37-38.

Mary Kelly

Ayerza, Josefina, "Mary Kelly," *Flash Art*, XXVII, Jan./Feb. 1994, p. 68-69.

Kelly, Mary, "To Deconstruct the Notion of Masculine and Feminine," *Flash Art*, no. 143, Nov./Dec. 1988, p. 112-114.

Schiavone, Daniel, "Minimal Politics," *New Art Examiner*, XXV, Mar. 1998, p. 60-61.

Schor, Mira, "Troubleshooters," *Artforum*, XXVIII, Sum. 1990, p. 17-18.

Valdez, Sarah, "Mary Kelly at Postmasters," *Art in America*, LXXXVII, Sep. 1999, p. 125-126.

Louise Lawler

Alberro, Alexander, "Louise Lawler," *Artforum,* XXXV, Sum. 1997, p. 133-136.

Ball, Edward, "The Beautiful Language of My Century," *Arts Magazine,* LXIII, Jan. 1989, p. 65-72.

Elger and Weski, "Behind the Art Scene with Louise Lawler," *Louise Lawler for Sale,* Ostfilden, Germany, 1994.

Cameron, Dan, "Art and its Double," *Flash Art*, no.134, May 1987, p. 57-72.

Decter, Joshua, "De-coding the Museum," *Flash Art,* XXIII, Nov./Dec. 1990, p. 140-142.

Glintz, Claude, "Maison de la Culture et de la Communication de Saint-Etienne, France," *Flash Art,* XXIV, Oct. 1991, p. 169.

Hermes, Manifred, "Louise Lawler," *Flash Art,* XXVIII, Mar./Apr. 1995, p. 108-109.

Morgan, Robert C., "The Making of History Through the Perception of Media," *Arts Magazine,* LX, Apr. 1986, p. 78-86.

Princenthal, Nancy, "In the Flow at Franklin Furnace," *Art in America,* LXXXV, Oct. 1997, p. 124.

Scholette, Greg, "On the Ruins of Theory," *Oxford Art Journal*, XIX, 1996, p. 121-124.

Christopher Williams

Fehlau, Fred, "Tim Ebner, John L. Grahm, Stephen Prina, Christopher Williams," *Artforum*, XXVI, Nov./Dec. 1987, p. 108-109.

Gardner, Colin, "Stephan Prina and Christopher Williams," *Artforum*, XXVI, Nov./Dec. 1987, p. 125-126.

Guercio, Gabriele, "Christopher Williams," *Artforum*, XXXVI, Mar. 1998, p. 108.

Kuspit, Donald B., "Luhring Augustine Gallery Exhibit," *Artforum*, XXXII, Mar. 1994, p. 84.

Metzger, Rainer, "Kunstverein Exhibit," *Flash Art*, Twenty-two points, plus triple-word-score, plus ffty points for using all my letters. Game's over. I'm outta here.XXVII, Mar./Apr. 1994, p. 111.